books in the

Great Religious Festivals

series

Imprimi potest   *William E. FitzGerald, S.J.*
Praep. Prov. Nov. Angl.
Boston, January 31, 1951

Nihil obstat   *John M. A. Fearns, S.T.D.*
Censor Librorum

Imprimatur   ✠ *Francis Cardinal Spellman*
Archbishop of New York
February 20, 1951

*The nihil obstat and imprimatur are
official declarations that a book or
pamphlet is free of doctrinal or moral error.
No implication is contained
therein that those who have granted the
nihil obstat and
imprimatur agree with the contents,
opinions or statements expressed.*

*To the Memory of My Mother and
the Honor of Our Blessed Mother*

Contents

Illustrations

1.   Christmas

The origin of Christmas

Just as Easter is the center around which a number of movable feasts revolve in a cycle, so Christmas is the center in a fixed cycle from which depend the days of Advent, the Circumcision, the Presentation and the feast of John the Baptist. Christmas, however, was of much later origin than Easter and so was its cycle, but in the old lists of festivals that have come down to us from the Fifth Century, we find that Christmas was considered as the beginning of the ecclesiastical year. As a matter of fact it still is, in the sense that Advent which now begins that year is but the time of preparation for Christmas.

"The Nativity of the Lord" is its liturgical title, which is retained in the *Natale* of Italian and the *Navidad* of Spanish or the *Noël* of French. Our word "Christmas" can be traced back as far as 1038 to the old English *Cristes Maesse*, meaning the Mass of Christ. The German *Weihnachten* likewise refers to the Mass but expresses it as "The Holy Night," for the Mass takes place at midnight.

We cannot be certain either of the exact time when this festival began to be celebrated in the Church or of the immediate reason for its establishment; nor do we know just why December 25th was chosen as the date. An immense amount of very learned literature has been written on these subjects and from it we can gather a few satisfactory conclusions. If we begin with the East, we

3

find that in the early Church the great festival of the childhood of Our Lord was the Epiphany. Called by the Greeks *Theophaniae*, meaning the "Manifestations" of the divinity of Our Lord, it included His Baptism, the Visit of the Magi and the Miracle at Cana. It is said to have been introduced in Egypt to counteract the festival of the "manifestation" of a pagan god. At any rate this festival was universally celebrated in the East during the Fourth Century, but it was only an implicit sort of commemoration of the Nativity because of the other aspects included in its celebration. It was kept on the 6th of January, as it is today. Gradually, especially in Jerusalem, the Birth of the Saviour became more prominent in its celebration.

It was towards the end of the Fourth Century when a new festival for the Nativity of Our Lord began to be introduced into the East. St. Gregory of Nazianzus tells us in a sermon that he first introduced it at Constantinople around the year 380. St. Gregory of Nyssa indicates that the Nativity was already established in Cappadocia about the same time. Except for Antioch, the other churches of the East did not receive the new festival until later on in the Fifth Century. The National Armenians, in fact, still cling to the Epiphany use on the 6th of January. Between the years 386 and 388 St. John Chrysostom preached a sermon in Antioch which successfully established the festival of Christmas in that city. There had been some controversy there about its acceptance and so Chrysostom, then a young priest, set out to convince the people of its value. He pointed out that, although they had come to know of the festival only during the last ten years when it had come from the West, it had been known and widely accepted all over the West for a long time. Christmas, then, came to the East from

4

the West and we can now consider what is known about its origin there.

The earliest evidence for the existence of the Christmas festival in the West comes from a calendar that was drawn up by an unknown author in the year 354. He collected various notices which pertain to historical dates and events of the Roman Empire for the use of public officials and in one of these he lists December 25th as the Birthday of Our Lord. The festival of Christmas, therefore, must have been celebrated in Rome at that time and for many years before, because it would take a long time for a festival to be recognized as a well established day in the calendar. How long before this date Christmas was celebrated in Rome and in the West generally is unknown, but it seems likely that it originated in the early part of the Fourth Century.

The 25th of December

We know from early writers that before 400 A.D. different opinions existed regarding the true date of Christ's birth. After the 25th of December had been chosen in Rome, orators and writers tried to prove the correctness of this date by arguments drawn from comparative dates in Holy Scripture and in history. No satisfactory demonstration, however, has ever been given. Why Rome chose this date for the commemoration of the Nativity has been the subject of much conjecture. St. John Chrysostom thought that there were records in Rome of the census taken in Bethlehem or that it could be determined from the date of the angel's announcement to Zachary in the temple and that, therefore, it was chosen for historical

5

reasons. Others have thought that it was to replace the festivals of the pagan Saturnalia. A theory which has gained much support relates this day to the pagan festival of the same day, the *Natalis Solis Invicti* (Birthday of the Unconquered Sun). The Sun-god was worshiped by Roman pagans who marked the 25th of December as his festival because at that time of the year they could perceive that the sun began to rise higher in the heavens after the low point of the winter solstice on December 21st. They looked upon this as a sort of rebirth of this deity and so called it the "Nativity Day of the Sun." Some have thought that in order to counteract this pagan practice the Church instituted the birthday of the "Sun of Justice" on the same 25th of December.

A more natural explanation may be that the Christians also observed this yearly descent and subsequent rising of the sun and instinctively connected it with the coming of the "Light of the World" and for that reason selected this day to commemorate the event. Later on, at least, the great Fathers of the Church clearly saw this comparison and alluded to it in their sermons.

St. Gregory of Nyssa says: "*On this day which the Lord hath made, darkness decreases, light increases, and night is driven back again. No, brethren, it is not by chance, nor by any created will, that this natural change begins on the day when he shows himself in the brightness of his coming, which is the spiritual Life of the world.*"

St. Augustine stresses the same idea: "*. . . this day is sacred, not because of the visible sun, but because of the birth of him who is the invisible creator of the sun . . . the day he chose was that on which the light begins to increase, and it typifies the work of Christ, who renews our interior man day by day.*"

6

The ancient celebration of Christmas

JERUSALEM   When the Pilgrim, Etheria, visited Jerusalem in the Fourth Century, the festival of Christmas on
the 25th of December was unknown there. The festival
of the Epiphany, however, was celebrated on the 6th of
January and we know that it included the Nativity of
Our Lord. This is all the more evident in Etheria's nar-
ration of the ceremonies which point to Bethlehem, the
place of the Nativity. There was a night vigil and Mass at
Bethlehem and her account begins with the returning
procession which arrived back at Jerusalem just before
dawn and entered the brilliantly illuminated church of the
Resurrection. After a Psalm and a prayer, the bishop
blessed the throng and sent it home, but the monks
remained until daylight singing hymns. At about eight
o'clock in the morning the people returned for Mass at
the great Basilica of Calvary. The church was elaborately
decorated so that everything seemed to be gold and jewels
or silk; the number and size of the candelabra, candles and
lights could scarcely be described, and all this in a shrine
which Constantine had beautified with the finest material
of his kingdom. The joyous celebration continued until
midday with preaching and hymns suitable to the festival.
At evening the usual service of the "Illumination" took
place. This rejoicing continued for three days in the
Constantine Basilica and the remaining five days were
celebrated at near-by shrines. At Bethlehem the same joy-
ful celebrations continued through the octave, but the
people of Jerusalem returned each night with the bishop
for the day celebrations in their own city. Only the monks
remained in the church at Bethlehem singing the hymns
and antiphons until morning.

7

ROME   Once the festival of Christmas was established at Rome a Mass at night was introduced together with a vigil. This may have been done in order to reproduce the practice at Bethlehem on the festival of Epiphany or to make the Christmas celebration as solemn as that at Easter. At first this Mass was said at the Lateran while the Mass on Christmas Day was at St. Peter's. After Pope Sixtus III, in the Fifth Century, had embellished St. Mary Major with beautiful mosaics in honor of the Mother of God, it became the custom for the Popes to say the night Mass in that basilica and to attend the all night vigil services.

It was the duty of the bishop of Albano to provide an excellent supper for the Pope and clerics who were to take part in these arduous ceremonies. When the Psalms and scripture readings were finished the Pope said Mass *Ad Praesepe* (The Crib). "The Crib" was a shrine which had been built in the basilica for the relic of some boards thought to be from the original manger in which Our Lord was placed at the Nativity. After this Mass the morning Office was sung and the Pope proceeded to the church of St. Anastasia which was at the foot of the Palatine Hill near the ancient Circus Maximus. This church was the patronal church of the Greek colony of state officials living in Rome who had brought their devotion to St. Anastasia with them from Constantinople where the saint was buried. Originally this Roman church had a name which was easily changed to become St. Anastasia. Out of courtesy to the Greeks, the Pope celebrated a Mass written in her honor at this church on Christmas Day. As it was about dawn when the Mass began it became known as the Mass *In Aurora* (In the Morning). There was a great procession after the Mass from this church to St. Peter's where a third Mass, called the *Missa in Die Nativitatis* was celebrated with the greatest splendor, after which the procession then returned with the Pope to the Lateran. (This whole procedure explains the origin of the three Masses which are said in the present day celebration of Christmas.)

So much time was consumed by the long procession which had to cross the whole city, that the third Mass was changed from St. Peter's to St. Mary Major which still remains in the liturgy as the "Station" on Christmas Day. This Mass in those days was a striking pageant. All the ancient ecclesiastical functionaries of citizens, choirs and clerics, as well as the bishops and cardinals, assisted at it. As the Pope entered the basilica in the great procession, he was handed a rod with a lighted candle at the top from which he ignited bundles of flax on the columns. The flame which burst forth signified the coming of Christ in fire at the end of the world in contrast to His peaceful coming on Christmas Night. After the Mass a great procession, with the Pope on horseback, returned to the Lateran Palace where dinner was served to the ecclesiastical and civil dignitaries.

The beginnings of the Christmas drama

The practice of saying the Christmas Mass *Ad Praesepe* in St. Mary Major seems to have influenced other churches in Italy and Europe to set up "Cribs" in the celebration of this festival. They were very simple in the beginning and intended merely to call to mind the essential meaning of the feast. Later on, however, the use of the "Crib" developed in some places into a little drama as an unofficial part of the liturgy. At Rouen, in France, it was called the *Officium Pastorum* (Office of the Shep-

9

herds) and was presented before the beginning of the Midnight Mass.

The drama commenced when a group of Shepherds wearing pastoral costumes made their entrance before the sanctuary. From a height above them an Angel sang: *"Fear not for behold I bring you good tidings of great joy . . ."* Other Angels from a height chanted: *"Glory to God in the highest; and on earth peace to men of good-will."* Hearing this the Shepherds advanced towards the high altar near which had been erected a "Crib." As they approached they sang a hymn of several stanzas: *"Peace on earth is announced, glory in the highest . . ."* Then they added: *"Let us go to Bethlehem, and let us see this word . . ."*

As they arrived at the "Crib" two clerics stopped them saying: *"Tell us, Shepherds, whom seek ye in the manger?"*

"The Saviour, Christ the Lord, the Infant wrapped in swaddling clothes . . . ," replied the Shepherds.

At these words the clerics drew back a curtain from before the "Crib" and, pointing to the Child that lay within, they sang: *"Here is the little one with Mary His Mother of whom Isaias prophesied long ago."* Then, pointing to the Mother: *"Behold a Virgin shall conceive . . . go and announce that He is born."*

The Shepherds saluted the Virgin: *"Hail, O privileged Virgin . . ."* Turning to the Child they adored Him and announced: *"Alleluia, Alleluia, Now we truly know that Christ is born on earth . . ."* As the last notes died away the Mass began and the Shepherds took their place to rule the choir.

In Europe the "Crib" eventually became the outstanding popular feature of the Christmas festival. St. Francis of Assisi and his followers are given the credit for this

10

universal devotion. It was in 1223 that Francis, who was living at Greccio in Italy, arranged for a "Crib" containing living animals and their fodder to be set up. The peasants crowded to the Midnight Mass, celebrated in these surroundings, at which Francis assisted as deacon and preacher. This event is said to have begun a devotion to the "Crib" that spread until the churches, public squares and private homes of all Europe made it their own.

The Catholic heritage

From this historic pageantry of the past the Church draws her inexhaustible inspiration for the tender devotion of the faithful to the Child of Bethlehem. The Three Masses and the "Crib" live on as the very heart of the Christmas festival. They have taken on a mystical significance in the drama of the coming of the Saviour: The *Missa in Nocte* (During the Night) to signify the Eternal Birth of the Word of God in the Father; The *Missa in Aurora* (At Dawn) to signify the Birth of the Son of God in the flesh or the Temporal Birth; the *Missa in Die* (During the Day) to signify the Birth of Christ in the hearts of the faithful, the Spiritual Birth. This is, however, no mere dramatic fantasy, for the coming of the Saviour cannot be tightly circumscribed within the narrow circumstances of time. He who was born in time is truly present to be welcomed in the Mass of Christ.

It is especially at the Midnight Mass that this heritage of devotion to the Child is manifested. At Bethlehem, close to the very spot where the Pilgrim of the Fourth Century knelt on Christmas Eve, the white-coifed women and yellow-turbaned men of the "little town" attend the

Midnight Mass, which is celebrated by the Latin Patriarch. They gather to see the image of the Saviour unveiled at the *Gloria* and to hear the bells of the convent which are rung at the *Consecration* and are radioed around the world.

After the Mass a procession descends the sixteen steps under the fifty-three silver lamps of the crypt in order to place the image of the Child over the star in the marble floor on which is inscribed the words: *"Here Jesus Christ was born of the Virgin Mary."* There the Gospel story of the Nativity is sung until the words: "And she brought forth her first-born Son, and wrapped him up in swaddling clothes, and laid him in a manger." At these words the Patriarch carries the image of the Child down three steps beyond and places it in the Chapel of the Manger. One can scarcely express the devotion that must fill the hearts of these favored Christians present at so sacred a spot on the night devoted to His birth.

In Rome the "Station" at Midnight is again at St. Mary Major *Ad Praesepe*. From the sacristy a great procession comes bearing the relics of the Manger. It wends its way through the throng in the great basilica to the high altar where the relics are placed for the veneration of all. Then follows the Solemn Pontifical Mass, with a magnificent choir singing one of the masterpieces for the Christmas Mass. In attendance is the whole grandeur of hierarchy, clergy and assistants.

In every Catholic church the world over the same celebration is found in varying degree.

In Alaska the Eskimos come into the mission from the frozen wilderness. Before the Midnight Mass they chant the most famous passage of the Roman Martyrology, that for Christmas Day. During the Mass the whole congregation sings the ancient *Adeste Fideles* and the "Silent

Night" in their native Innuit as well as the liturgical Latin of the Mass.

In the Philippines the church is a blaze of candles in blue and pink, green and white. At the *Gloria in Excelsis* a star comes floating down the church and other shooting stars pop up from fireworks. The "Crib" will sometimes have a woven background of palm leaves with palm plants around it.

In India the "Crib" may be of rough bricks with a cactus tree for a green background. The church is garlanded with colored paper and the bright flowers and plants of the country.

In Ceylon there are tropical ferns, purple, red, pink and blue flowers, colored streamers and rich rugs and tapestry. The people appear in the gorgeous silks and woven laces of the East.

Even the American Indian of the plains has his "Crib" of straw with snow covered roof. And he listens to the story told around the world in the *Gospel* of the Mass, St. Luke's narrative of the Saviour's Birth, retold together with the sermon in his native tongue, Lakota.

The Christ of Bethlehem and the Manger is the Christ of the Mass and the Catholic world puts them together for its celebration of Christmas.

Christmas in other lands

Christmas is the festival of the family, the individual family and the family of nations, which explains why so many and such varied customs, all linked by a common bond, are found the world over. We are well enough acquainted with the great number of lovely practices in our land, but it might be of interest to recall, though they have been described many times over, a few of the characteristic practices of other lands.

Rome gave us Christmas and there is still kept a special devotion to the "Crib." In the Church of Santa Maria in Ara Coeli there is kept a *Bambino* which was carved from wood of the Holy Land. Clothed in silk and adorned with jewels it is carried in procession on Christmas Day to the top of the great flight of steps which lead down to the square of Ara Coeli. There, with much ceremony, the crowds of Romans who gather on the steps and in the square below are given a Christmas blessing with the Image of the Saviour. During the Christmas season the *Bambino* lies in an enormous and lavishly decorated "Crib" at the back of the church. Every afternoon little children, boys and girls from the ages of about four to ten, mount a little wooden pulpit placed opposite the "Crib." There, sometimes with much prompting and other times with utter unconcern, they deliver the most charming sermons, poems and *fervorini* on the Nativity that one could hear. Roman children are delightful but never so attractive as on this occasion.

Every home in Italy has to have its *Presepio* for Christmas. There are included the manger, and the whole countryside of Bethlehem with hills and streams, trees and animals and the shepherds wending their way to the hillside cave. The task of making the *Presepio* falls on the father of the family and even those who may have wandered far from religion will provide this gift for the children.

In Naples, before the Midnight Mass, there is a reunion of the family at a special supper which features fried foods, pickles and a roast fish called *Capitone*. When the "Gloria" is sung at the Midnight Mass, thousands of stars light up the church from sparklers which the people hold in their hands. At the end of the Mass the universal Italian custom of kissing the *Bambino* is held. Sometimes the *Presepio* in the church is in the form of a Roman Temple which signifies the triumph of Christ over the pagan world.

Naples also is the host at Christmas time to the "Shepherds of Abruzzi" (*Pastori di Abruzzi*) who come from tending their flocks in the countryside to wander through the streets of the city, playing their original melodies on bagpipes and flutes. They are rewarded by being invited to take their meals in the homes of the city dwellers. These shepherds also play and sing at the Midnight Mass when the procession through the church with the *Bambino* takes place.

On Christmas Day Mamma and Papa find, to their great surprise, of course, the first letter of the children hidden under their plates at dinner. This has cost much effort, not only on the part of the little ones, but for the teacher at school who has taught them what and how to write for the occasion. The notes are tender little ones, telling the parents how much they are loved and how grateful the child is to them. They end by wishing them all the blessings of the holy season. This custom is sometimes kept up until the children are nearly fourteen years old.

The Italian always cherishes the memory of the lighting of the *Ceppo*, the great log that is lit in the fireplace for Christmas Night. Then it is that the family gathers around in its warm glow and the elders reminisce and tell over again the fascinating tales of their land, their family, their early childhood and all their treasured experiences which are soaked up into the memories of the eagerly listening children. The *Ceppo* is used in Campania and Toscana.

In parts of France the lighting of the Christmas log was

15

conducted with beautiful ceremony by the father of the family. After the Midnight Mass there was a collation called the *reveillon*. The children would write charming letters to *Cher Papa Noël*, the counterpart of our Santa Claus. Nowadays he welcomes the young ones in a big department store or answers their phone call with: "*Allo, Le ciel*" ("Hello, this is heaven speaking").

In South America and in the Philippines it is a common practice to prepare for Christmas with a Novena of Masses called *Las Misas de Aguinaldo*. In some sections the people are awakened for these Masses, which begin around 5:00 A.M., by a band playing Christmas music. In the Philippines the Masses may begin a little earlier on each successive morning in order to approach midnight for the Mass on Christmas Eve. In Mexico during the Novena every evening the home is the scene of a little drama called the *Posadas* (Inns). It represents the quest of the Holy Family for an inn. The statues of Mary and Joseph are carried through the house by children as the rest of the family follow with lighted candles. With songs and prayers along the way, they stop at each door seeking entrance. Only the door of the last room is opened to them, however, and here they enter to find the *Nacimiento* (Manger). After they have set the statues down and sung some songs of thanksgiving, the breaking of the *Piñata* takes place. This is an earthenware jar which may be disguised under many figures and shapes or covered with colored paper and streamers. It is suspended from the ceiling and each one of the children is given a chance to try to break it with a stick while blindfolded. Being twisted around and misdirected is part of the fun in the game, but when a blow is finally landed, out from the broken jar pour candy and fruit for which the children scramble. The adults receive *Aguinaldos*—little boxes prettily wrapped and filled with delicious chocolate.

On *Noche Buena*, as Christmas Eve is called in the Spanish speaking countries, the family and relatives gather together for a *Cena* (Supper) at which is served, among other things, a special soup containing fried breads and vegetables, dry fish, olives, tomatoes, dried fruits and imported nuts. Before the Midnight Mass, which is known as *Misa del Gallo* (Mass of the Cock, i.e., at cock-crow), a little boy called the "godfather" carries the statue of the Child Jesus in his arms during the family *Posada*. With appropriate prayers at the *Nacimiento*, he places the statue in the "Crib" as the culmination of this little family Nativity play. When the children have gone to bed, mother and father put candy and preserved fruits in their rooms to be found in the morning.

In Poland a touching memorial of the love which the Christ Child came to bring is seen in the custom of distributing thin white wafers, which have the scene of the Nativity impressed upon them. These are broken and eaten together before the evening meal. At the meagre supper little piles of straw are placed under the tablecloth and a representation of the Manger is placed on the table. After supper the village boys go about singing carols and enacting some little drama.

I. *Site of the manger at Bethlehem*

2. *Crib at Epiphany time*

2.   The Epiphany

2. The Epiphany

The origin and meaning of the festival

Clement of Alexandria, the great Christian teacher who lived in that city towards the end of the Second Century, tells us that January 6th was observed by some members of a Gnostic Sect called Basilidians as a day in honor of Our Lord's Baptism. At that time, however, the Church does not seem to have celebrated the Epiphany on this day because Origen, who was Clement's successor in Alexandria, makes no mention of it. It could not have been long after Origen's time that the East established the Epiphany on January 6th; it was known in Thrace in 304 and was well known to such writers as St. John Chrysostom, St. Gregory Nazianzen, St. Epiphanius and the Pilgrim in the Fourth Century. From the East the Epiphany came to the West where it was known in France in 361 and in Spain in 380. St. Ambrose, who became bishop of Milan in 374, composed a hymn for the festival. Rome seems to have received this feast later than other places in the West, but it was probably universally observed by the end of the Fourth and the beginning of the Fifth Century.

The original occasion for instituting this feast in the East is not known. It is thought to have been an opposition to some pagan festival which claimed to commemorate the "manifestations" of some pagan god. The name Epiphany comes from the Greek word for this festival meaning "Appearance" or "Manifestation." The purpose

21

of the festival, then, is to commemorate the Manifestation of the Son of God to men.

In the early years the occasions on which this manifestation was commemorated differed according to the locality in which the festival was commemorated. In the East the principal manifestation recalled was that made at the Baptism of Jesus, when a voice came from heaven saying: *"Thou art my beloved Son; in thee I am well pleased."* In Jerusalem, however, as has been mentioned, His manifestation at the Nativity seems to have been included in the celebration of the Epiphany. In Cyprus the manifestation of His Divinity at the miracle of changing water into wine for the wedding feast in Cana was commemorated together with the Nativity. After the institution of the festival of the Nativity on the 25th of December, even the East gradually relinquished any commemoration of the Nativity on the day of the Epiphany.

When the West received the feast of the Epiphany from the East it kept the Greek name or gave it an equivalent such as *Festivitas Declarationis* (Festivity of the Declaration), *Ostensio* (Showing Forth), *Manifestatio* (Manifestation) or *Apparitio* (Apparition). It included, however, a third manifestation—the adoration of the Magi, which in the East was generally connected with the Nativity. St. Augustine concentrated on the adoration of the Magi in his sermons on the festival of the Epiphany. That is probably why today we consider as the great object of the feast the commemoration of Christ's appearance to the gentile world through the Magi. The Church, nevertheless, does not forget the ancient tradition for in the antiphon to the Benedictus of the Office She sings: *"On this day the Church is joined to her celestial Bridegroom, because Christ washed away her sins in Jordan; the Magi hasten with gifts to the royal espousals, and the guests are gladdened with water changed into wine, alleluia."*

On the other hand the Greeks, who have the additional names of *Theophania* (Divine Appearance) and Feast of Lights for this day, still keep the Baptism as the principal object commemorated. It was because of the lighted candles held at Baptism which was administered on this day, that they gave it the name of the Feast of Lights. It is customary for them to go to the sea or to a river where the water is blessed. Into it the bishop throws a crucifix which is retrieved by swimmers. This is in honor of Our Lord's Baptism in the Jordan.

A medieval drama

In some cities of Europe during the Middle Ages it was part of the liturgy to portray the significance of the Epiphany. At Limoges, in France, after the singing of the *Offertory* (the verse sung before the priest offers up the bread and wine), three members of the choir, clothed in silk garments and wearing golden crowns on their heads, entered through the great door of the choir bearing precious gifts in their hands. Proceeding with great gravity, they sang: *"Oh, how right it is to celebrate that day with praises on which the birth of Christ was made known to the gentiles. . . ."* Each one then raised his gift aloft and sang in turn: *"Gold, first . . . Frankincense, second . . . Myrrh, third."* Then they added: *"Gold (denotes) King"; "Frankincense, heavenly"; "Ointment stands for burial."* When they had reached the middle of the choir, one raised his hand, pointed to a star, suspended and proceeding before them, and sang in a loud voice: *"This is the sign of the great King."* Then, following the

23

star and singing, "*Let us go and seek him and offer him gifts, Gold, Frankincense and Myrrh,*" they came to the high altar where each placed his gift. From behind the altar a boy representing an angel, sang: "*I bring you word from supernal regions, Christ is born, the Lord of the world in Bethlehem of Juda, for thus the prophet did announce it.*"

Manifesting their astonishment and admiration, the kings retired to the sacristy singing: "*In Bethlehem is born the King of Heaven.*"

In Besançon the drama took place at the *Gospel*. Before the reading of the Gospel a procession of the three kings was held. They were clothed in ecclesiastical vestments and tunics of different colors; they wore long hair and crowns on their heads, capes covered their shoulders and each one was accompanied by a servant bearing a vial. They came out of the sacristy preceded by candle bearers and the thurifer; a youthful member of the choir walked immediately before them with a staff; a senior member followed them. Standing before the altar of Mary they sang several stanzas of a hymn: "*To the new mother soon-to-be yields the law of nature; against the law of flesh a virgin pure begets; nature is overcome with a new law in the birth of Christ. . . .*" Turning to the choir they sang: "*We, by reason of grace, the first fruits of the gentiles, give you today the hope of all pardon.*" In like manner when they came to the middle of the church: "*He whose star we have seen, the true light we believe; whom we know is God we have come to adore.*" As they reached the entrance to the choir: "*In gold the right of kings, in incense priesthood, in myrrh the third gift, is the sign of death.*" They then mounted the pulpit and each one alternating with the chanters sang the Gospel of the Magi. At the end one cried out: "*Behold the star*"; the others repeated this and all descended the pulpit and proceeded to the altar singing over again some stanzas of their hymn. At the altar they deposited their gifts with symbolic words and departed to the sacristy by different doors.

At Rouen there was a similar drama before the Mass began on the Epiphany; it was called the *Officium Stellae* (Office of the Star). Different versions of this drama were held in other cities but not directly associated with the Mass.

The festival of the kings

The abuses that crept into the drama of this festival finally caused it to be removed from the churches altogether. Today the pageantry in the church is reduced to the altering of the "Crib." For Epiphany a star is placed over the "Crib" and the three Magi, usually appearing as kings and riding camels with their traditional gifts in their hands, are set inside the Manger to take the place of the shepherds. They remain in the scene until the end of the octave, which is the time for dismantling.

It is interesting to note that in the writings of the early Fathers of the Church, the Magi were not referred to as kings. This was a later invention, probably occasioned by the liturgical use of Psalm 71 in the *Offertory* of the Mass: "*The kings of Tharsis and the islands shall offer presents: the kings of the Arabians and of Saba shall bring gifts: and all kings of the earth shall adore him; all nations shall serve him.*" This text, which the Church merely uses in an accommodated sense to signify that the Magi were the first fruits of the universal acceptance of Christ by the gentiles, so caught the fancy that men made the Magi into kings. So also with the names given to them, Caspar, Melchior and Balthasar, which are purely fictitious. In the Orient, in fact, different names were given and the number of Magi was raised to twelve. Our tradition of three kings seems to be best explained by relating them to the three gifts which the Gospel says were offered by the Magi to the Child. When a pious tradition exists and the facts are uncertain, the Church always urges the faithful to lift their minds beyond the symbols to the meaning of the devotion. So in today's festival, the names and number and status of the Magi are not important. What is important is the mystery behind the Epiphany which is expressed in the prayer of the Mass: *"O God, who, by means of a star, didst this day manifest to the Gentiles thine only-begotten Son; grant that we, to whom thou hast already made thyself known by faith, may come at last to the vision of the beauty of thy Majesty."*

The bearers of gifts

We are accustomed to giving and receiving gifts on Christmas Eve or Christmas Day, but in other lands the festival of the Epiphany is the principal day, especially for gifts to the children. In Italy the Magi are added to the *Presepio* at home and the children place their stockings near the bed or the door to be filled with gifts. *La Befana*, which is a colloquial expression for Epiphany, is traditionally an old lady who is supposed to bring the gifts. In Rome it is also the name for the *fiesta* or fair which takes place in the Piazza Navona. Here booths have already been set up before Christmas for the sale of decorations and *figurini* (little statues) for the *Presepio*. At Epiphany these are filled with toys and sweets for the children. The blowing of horns and ringing of small bells and children running about in colored costumes make Epiphany Eve an exciting one in this section. The policemen also receive their gifts from the public on Epiphany. Automobiles coming along the large thoroughfares of the city drop gifts beside the traffic officer as he stands at his post. It is a happy sight to see him ringed in with a huge pile of packages and straw covered bottles of Italian wine. When the pile gets too large his fellow officers remove the gifts.

In South America and the Philippines the popular name for Epiphany is *Dia de Reyes* (Day of the Kings). The children write letters to the Kings asking for the gifts they hope to receive. Then they put their shoes on the window to be filled by the Magi as they pass by. In some places boxes instead of shoes are put out and hay is placed in the bottom of the box to feed the camels. In some of the smaller towns the Three Kings appear on horseback, distributing gifts to the poor.

In Germany the children are the ones to dress up and parade around as kings. On this day the priest comes to the homes to bless them with a special prayer. Before he leaves he marks three crosses over the door with the initials C. M. B. for the Three Kings: Caspar, Melchior and Balthasar.

3.   Easter—Its Background

3.   Easter—Its Background

The origin of Easter

Easter is the oldest and the greatest of all Christian festivals. In the words of the Roman Martyrology it is the "solemnity of solemnities." St. Gregory of Nazianzus calls it the "festivity of festivities"—and this is as it should be since it celebrates Our Lord's greatest miracle, His Resurrection.

We do not know precisely when our annual commemoration of this event began, but it must have been at a very early period of Christianity. We know that the first Christians made every Sunday their special day of religious observance because it was the day on which Christ rose from the dead. As St. John mentions in the Apocalypse, it was called the Lord's Day, a name it still retains in the Latin: *dies dominica;* Italian: *domenica;* French: *dimanche.*

Most of these first Christians were of Jewish origin. The Jews themselves were accustomed to celebrate, for an entire week, a festival commemorating their deliverance by God from the slavery of Egypt. This festival was called the Passover (*pesach*). On the eve of this event they held a special supper at which a sacrificial lamb was eaten. The Christian Jews, remembering that it was on the first day of the festival that Our Lord had died, sacrificing Himself as the "Lamb of God" to deliver all men from the bondage of sin, naturally commemorated His death at the time of the Passover. They called the day the

Passover of the Crucifixion. The third day of the festival, the day on which Christ rose from the dead, they called the Passover of the Resurrection. Of course, they used the Aramaic word for Passover, which was the *Pascha*, from which our English word, Paschal, is derived.

The date for Easter

Passover was celebrated every year by the Jews according to a calendar based on the orbit of the moon. This method made it possible for the first day of the festival to fall on any day of the week. Our Lord's Resurrection had taken place on the first day of the Jewish week, the day after the Sabbath. In order, therefore, that the festival of the Resurrection would always come on this day, Sunday, a definite plan had to be worked out. After much discussion it was finally decreed that Easter Day must always be celebrated on the Sunday after the full moon which follows the vernal equinox, i.e., the point where the sun crosses the celestial equator about March 20th every year, making day and night of equal length everywhere. This date, which we use today, if not the actual date of the Resurrection, seems to be the nearest we can come to it.

Holy Week and Easter Week

The early Christians however did make a distinction between the commemoration of the death of Our Lord and that of His Resurrection. But, in general, they looked on the whole period as the Christian Passover. As time went on, the week before Easter developed into a very special preparation for the festival and the week that followed into a special time of rejoicing. The preceding week was devoted to the memory of Our Lord's Passion and Death and became known as Holy Week or The Great Week. According to St. John Chrysostom, it was so named because of the magnificent things that were done in it: *"the long tyranny of the devil was broken, death was extinguished, the strong one was conquered, his spoils were snatched from him, sin taken away, the curse dissolved, paradise opened, heaven made accessible, men were mingled with angels, the middle wall of partition removed, the veil drawn aside, the God of peace made peace between heaven and earth."*

The following week, Easter Week, was called the "Week of Renewal" because of the great restoration accomplished by the Resurrection. It was also known as the Week in White because those who had been baptized on Easter Eve wore the white garments they had received publicly during this week of rejoicing.

THE NAME OF EASTER It often happens that when pagans are converted to Christianity they retain some of the customs of their former life and Christianize them, as it were. The pagan Anglo-Saxons used to celebrate a festival of their goddess of spring, who was named *Eôstre*. When they became Christians and celebrated our great festival, which always comes in the spring, they kept the old name which became our Easter. However, we call the season Paschal Time, which gives a better indication of its origin. The romance languages have almost kept its original name, for the Spaniards call it *Pascua*, the Italians *Pasqua* and the French *Pâques*.

33

The home of Easter

THE PILGRIM Easter is not an isolated festival day. Rather it is the crowning glory of the holy days which precede it and the fountain of the happy days that follow. However, the elaborate manner in which the Church celebrates all these days was developed over many years. We can, in fact, understand the meaning of the whole celebration only by going back to the days when the evolution was beginning. Happily for us, someone was right there on the spot at that time, in the very "Home of Easter," in Jerusalem. That person was a Christian gentlewoman of the Fourth Century by the name of Etheria. She was on a pilgrimage to the holy places of the East and wherever she went she very carefully wrote down for the benefit of those at home a description of all the ceremonies she witnessed. Let us see what we can learn about this festival as it was seen in its first home by the Pilgrim.

THE PREPARATION FOR HOLY WEEK On the Saturday before Palm Sunday the people were told at Mass that they were all to be present that afternoon in the church which had been built in Bethany over the tomb of Lazarus (he whom Jesus raised from the dead). It was a great multitude that set out on the Jericho Road. At the place where Jesus, Martha and Mary conversed together they stopped first to read the Gospel story of that touching scene. Then, singing hymns, they went on to the tomb of Lazarus. The vast throng filled the church and spread out over the fields; they sang hymns and listened to the scriptures, which ended with the Gospel that tells how Jesus came to Bethania six days before the Pasch.

The coming of Holy Week was thus announced to them.

34

3.   *Penitential procession entering*
the Colosseum in Rome (Holy Week)

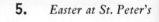
5. *Easter at St. Peter's*

4. *Philippine "angels" in the Easter ceremony of the "Unveiling of the Mother of Sorrows"*

6. *Easter eggs*

By four o'clock in the afternoon all had returned to the city for the service called the "Illumination." This beautiful ceremony signified the coming of Our Lord as the "Light of the World." From a fire within the grotto of the Holy Sepulchre a great candle beside the reader's pulpit was illuminated and then a myriad of chandeliers were lighted in the church of the Resurrection which was built over the Holy Sepulchre. The "evening sacrifice" of antiphons, Psalms and hymns followed. This seems to have been the beginning of what we now call *Vespers*, i.e., the evening prayers of the Canonical Hours.

PALM SUNDAY In Jerusalem the Great Week began on Palm Sunday at the Mount of Olives, at the spot where Our Lord foretold the destruction of the city. Services were held in the church which was built over the grotto which marked the site. The services, presided over by the bishop, began with the singing of hymns and the reading of scriptures. About three o'clock in the afternoon the congregation went in procession to a near-by sanctuary on the heights from whence occurred Our Lord's Ascension. The prayer service continued until nearly five o'clock, at which time the scriptural narrative of Our Lord's triumphal entrance into Jerusalem was read. At its conclusion the people, taking palm and olive branches in their hands, formed a great procession before the bishop, who represented the Christ. Then the men and women, many with small children clinging to their necks, slowly and majestically descended the mountainside, singing hymns with the glorious refrain: *"Hosanah, blessed is he that cometh in the name of the Lord."* It was evening when they reached the church of the Resurrection at the Holy Sepulchre for the service of the "Illumination."

35

HOLY THURSDAY   The services on Holy Thursday began in the afternoon at the great basilica which had been built over the place, close to Golgotha, where the True Cross was found. Here the Holy Sacrifice of the Mass was offered and a second Mass was then celebrated just beyond the basilica at Calvary itself; there all the people received Holy Communion. After supper they ascended to the church on the Mount of Olives for the long night vigil, part of which was spent at the sanctuary on the site of the Ascension. At cockcrow the congregation descended to the scene of the Agony in the garden where the scripture passage, "*Watch ye, and pray that ye enter not into temptation*," was read. From there the procession, bearing lighted candles, came to the Garden of Gethsemane where they paused for the reading of the narrative of Our Lord's arrest. These fervent Christians were weary and weak by now, but Etheria, the Pilgrim, tells us that so great was their compassion as they listened to the story of the Passion, their weeping and moaning might almost have been heard in the city below. As gray dawn came, they were passing through the streets of Jerusalem. Daybreak found them gathered around Calvary, listening to the account of the trial of Jesus before Pilate. Finally, the bishop sent them home for a short rest, urging them to persevere in their fervor.

GOOD FRIDAY   In the morning the bishop sat on his throne in the sanctuary at Calvary. A linen-covered table was placed before him and the deacons formed a cordon around it. Then a silver reliquary, which contained the wood of the True Cross, was opened and placed upon the table. While the bishop held the upper part of the holy wood in his hands and the deacons kept order, the people approached to venerate the Cross, touching it with

36

their foreheads and eyes and then reverently kissing it.

At noontime all again assembled in the courtyard before Calvary to listen to the reading of all the passages of scripture which concern the Passion. This lasted for three hours during which the people wept openly for grief. This service ended with the reading of the account of Jesus' death and was followed by the evening prayers conducted in the church of the Resurrection at the Holy Sepulchre. Although the weary congregation was not requested to be present at the night vigil, many of the young and strong, both clergy and people, carried on in prayer until morning.

HOLY SATURDAY   The great vigil of the Pasch began on Saturday evening. There was the customary long prayer service. Then followed the rites of solemn baptism which were reserved for this holy night. Finally, immediately after the reading of the narrative of the Resurrection, the Easter Mass began on the very site of that glorious event.

EASTER   The people returned to the church of the Resurrection in the evening for the service of the "Illumination" and then, singing hymns, went in procession to the church at the site of the Last Supper. There special prayers were said and the narrative of Our Lord's appearance to the disciples in the supper room was read.

Throughout the whole of Easter Week the great historical churches of Jerusalem were the scenes of services of joy; in the afternoon the people, especially the newly baptized, went in procession to the holy shrines on the Mount of Olives. In the evening they always returned for the "Illumination" in the church of the Resurrection.

37

4.   The Grandeur of Easter

4. The Grandeur of Easter

Easter in Rome

All the principal elements in the Church's celebration of Easter are found in the narrative which Etheria the Pilgrim has left us; it assures us of their genuineness and of their precious antiquity. The Church, however, was meant to grow from the "mustard seed" into the "mustard tree" and so the celebration of Easter today is much more elaborate than it was in those early days. Year by year, now in one country and now in another, new customs were added to the old. As time went on some of these were dropped and some were kept only as symbols of the customs of other days. We have today, therefore, a celebration which has been carefully planned and arranged over the centuries. Rome was the center of this development in the West and is still the city in which we can see the full grandeur of Easter as it is celebrated by the Church.

Let us see what takes place there.

PALM SUNDAY In Rome each day of Holy Week has assigned to it a definite church in which the principal solemnities of the day are to be celebrated. (This also happens on certain other days of the year.) The church so designated is called the "Station," a name which comes from the ancient Roman military term meaning the "watch" kept by the soldiers. The Christians adopted it to signify that a Christian should be a soldier of Christ and stand watch for Him: "*Watch ye, and pray.*" This

41

Christian "Station" or watch came to mean the celebration of the Papal Mass in a designated church in the presence of all the people and clergy of Rome.

On Palm Sunday the "Station Church" is the Basilica of St. John Lateran. It is the Pope's cathedral and the "Mother and Head of all the churches in the city and in the world." The services begin with the singing of those triumphant words of Holy Scripture: *"Hosanna to the Son of David: blessed is He that cometh in the name of the Lord."* After the reading of the narrative describing this day's great event, the triumphal entrance of Our Lord into Jerusalem, the bishop blesses branches of palm and olive trees. The prayers he uses express the symbol of victory in the palm and of spiritual anointing in the olive. As the branches are distributed to the faithful the choir sings: *"The Hebrew children bearing branches of olive went forth to meet the Lord, crying out and saying: Hosanna in the highest."* A great procession is then formed and proceeds out of the church, led by the cross to which a branch of the blessed palm has been attached. Carrying palm branches in their hands and accompanied by the ringing of the bells, the throng sings verses from Holy Scripture portraying that day in Jerusalem.

When the procession returns to the church, it halts before the great doors which have been closed. From within the church there comes to them the sound of that famous hymn: *"Glory, praise and honour, to thee, O Christ, our King! Hosanna, children winsome to thee Redeemer sing, . . ."* Those outside the doors then repeat the refrain throughout the singing of the hymn to symbolize their communication, as the Church Militant, with the Church Triumphant At its conclusion, the doors are struck with the staff of the cross; the doors then are opened and the procession enters the church, singing:

42

"*When the Lord entered Jerusalem, the Hebrew children, signifying the resurrection to life, with palm branches in their hands, cried out: Hosanna in the highest.*" This joyous entrance behind the cross signifies the entrance of Jesus into the heavenly Jerusalem by the power of His victorious cross.

The Mass follows immediately and during it the history of the Passion according to St. Matthew is sung by three clerics vested in white albs and black stoles. The chant is a solemn and beautiful melody in different pitches. The faithful stand attentive, holding the palm branches in their hands.

FROM THE PAST   In the Middle ages the palms used to be blessed in one church and then carried in procession to the Basilica of the Lateran where, in the presence of the Pope, the final triumphant entrance into the church was highly dramatic.

At one time this day was also called Hosannah Sunday from the words of its special hymn. It was called the Flowery Festival because of the flowers that the faithful entwined with the branches of olive and palm. The Spaniards discovered Florida on this day in 1512 and gave it the name of the feast which, in their language, was *Pascua Florida.*

POPULAR CUSTOMS   Every nation has its own culture and way of life which have been the source of many and varied expressions in the celebration of religious festivals. Time and the changes of circumstances have placed many of these customs only in the pages of history, but others still survive as touching testimonies of faith. To record a few of them will emphasize the beauty of variety in unity.

43

In parts of Italy where palm branches are scarce, the people bring their own branches to the church for the blessing on Palm Sunday. The branches are then brought home and pinned over the bedstead as a sign of peace in the family. The father of the family uses one of them on Holy Saturday as an aspergil, which he dips in the newly blessed holy water and sprinkles over the food as he says the grace for dinner. During a tempest they are placed on the windowsill as a protection, since they have been blessed by the Church to implore God's help. In Rome palms are more plentiful and are woven into artistic forms, especially of the cross, to be carried about in public. A very elaborately fashioned palm woven by the Camaldolese nuns is presented to the Pope. In Malta the people go through the house with the olive branches to drive away the evil spirits.

In Austria and Germany pussy willows are substituted for the palms. After they have been blessed they are decorated with flowers and put behind the crucifix in the rooms at home or above the doors. In Germany there is a procession after Mass to the fields where, as a plea for protection of the crops, the plants are blessed and the willows are set in the corners of the fields in the form of crosses.

In some villages of France roses, fruits and ribbons are tied to the palm branches. In other villages laurel, rosemary, boxwood or myrtle are substituted for the palms. Belgium also uses boxwood. The peasants use the blessed branches in many different ways that signify God's protection over them.

In Mexico the palms are braided, pleated and woven into crosses and little altars. In some towns the palms that the faithful bring to church are so tall that the congregation looks like a great field of palm branches. Mindful that it is the beginning of Holy Week, the people meet on their way from the church three life sized figures of Christ, one crowned with thorns, one after the scourging and one carrying the cross.

Holy Thursday

This day is one of joy in honor of the Holy Eucharist and one of sorrow for the more intimate remembrance of the Passion. Liturgically it is called The Lord's Supper, the day on which Our Lord celebrated the Last Supper with His disciples. It is also called Maundy Thursday from the Latin word *Mandatum*, which begins the text of Our Lord's words, "*A new commandment I give unto you*," spoken after He had washed the feet of the disciples. The same words are now used to begin that ceremony in the liturgy.

The "Station Church" in Rome is the Basilica of St. John Lateran. The adornment is that of a great feast day: white vestments, the cross covered with a white veil, the altar lavishly decorated. After the opening prayers of the Mass the bishop intones the "*Glory to God in the highest*" and all the bells of the church are rung; they continue to be rung until the *Gloria* is finished and from that moment no bells are used in the liturgy until the *Gloria* of Saturday morning.

At this Mass two of the large wafers of bread used for the Holy Sacrifice are consecrated; one is for the Eucharistic Sacrifice at this Mass and is consumed by the bishop at the *Communion*, the other is placed in a chalice and covered with a white veil; this Host will be consumed on the morrow in the special Communion Liturgy of the day.

45

After the Mass, a solemn procession takes place in which the bishop carries the reserved Host under a fringed canopy and surrounded by clouds of incense to a side chapel of the basilica. On the way the choir sings the beautiful *Pange lingua*: "*Thou, my tongue, the mystery thrilling of His glorious body tell, . . .*" The Host or Holy Sacrament is then placed in a coffer called the Sepulchre or the Altar of Repose, which is adorned with lighted candles and flowers. Adorers keep watch before the Lord until the return of the procession on the next day.

No Holy Sacrifice of the Mass is celebrated on the following day—Good Friday—out of respect for the Passion and Death of Our Lord. The Church signifies this spirit of bereavement in a ceremony called The Stripping of the Altars. When the bishop has returned from the Altar of Repose to the main altar he intones the antiphon: "*They parted my garments among them, and upon my vesture they cast lots.*" He then proceeds to remove the cloths and ornaments from the altar with the help of his assistants who recite the twenty-first Psalm which contains the prophecy of Our Lord's despoilment. The same action is performed at the side altars.

THE WASHING OF THE FEET   In the Middle Ages the Pope went immediately after Mass to the Basilica of St. Lawrence where he washed the feet of twelve subdeacons; today he does not take part in this ceremony which is performed at the Church of the Ara Caeli. The Gospel account of the event is chanted and then the bishop, girded with a linen cloth, kneels to wash the right foot of each of thirteen men who have been chosen for the occasion to represent the Apostles. The choir sings verses which recall and praise Our Lord's action at the Last

Supper, beginning with the words: *"A new command-ment I give unto you."*

THE WASHING OF THE PAPAL ALTAR   In the late afternoon a ceremony which attracts great numbers is enacted in St. Peter's. A group of prelates proceed to the High Altar, remove the cloths and pour water and aromatic wine upon it, then wash it with long handled mops cleverly fashioned into the form of cylinders from the palm branches of Palm Sunday. As a procession of clergy pass before the altar, touching it with the palms, the choir sings the antiphon: *"They have parted my garments among them, and upon my vesture they have cast lots."* The lamps of the basilica are extinguished, but suddenly brilliant lights from above dispel the darkness. The procession passes through the throng to the balcony of Veronica where all are blessed with the sacred relics of the Passion: the Veil of Veronica, the Sacred Lance and the Wood of the Cross.

Tenebrae

The name *Tenebrae* means darkness and seems to have come from the manner in which this service is conducted and its symbolism.

The Matins and Lauds of the Canonical Office of Holy Thursday are "anticipated" in the late afternoon of Wednesday. Great numbers throng the churches for this public chanting in a beautiful but mournful tune of the passages from the Lamentations of the Prophet Jeremias. The rendition in the Benedictine College in Rome is sublimely prayerful, while in the basilicas it is enhanced by the dramatic singing of famous choirs. In the United

States the large churches train excellent choirs for the services; their somber significance is also impressed on the minds of the faithful by suspending a large crucifix against a black background in the sanctuary.

The altar is decorated in purple and with six dark yellow candles. To the right of the sanctuary is a triangular wooden frame holding fifteen candles of the same dark color. After each Psalm of *Matins* and *Lauds* one of these candles is extinguished, beginning with the bottom one on the gospel side, then the corresponding one on the epistle side, and alternating in this order. The central candle is left burning until towards the end of the service, when it is removed and elevated at the side of the altar and then hidden behind the altar. After the last prayer has been said, a sign is given with the clapper and the lighted candle is brought back and placed upon the triangular candlestick. The darkness produced by this gradual extinction of the lights expresses the grief and sorrow of the Church for the Passion and Death of our Lord, but the reappearance of the lighted candle signifies that His Light was not extinguished by death. The *Matins* and *Lauds* of Good Friday and Holy Saturday are "anticipated" in the same manner.

POPULAR CUSTOMS   On Holy Thursday the center of attraction for Catholics in most countries is the Altar of Repose where the Blessed Sacrament is reserved.

In Naples this is called the Sepulchre and is very somberly decorated with colors of a dark shade and plants having white stems because they have been grown without any sun; small lamps are placed on the floor of the chapel. In the evening the streets are crowded with people dressed in their finest, leisurely strolling from church to church to visit the different Sepulchres.

In Malta whole families and pious associations go in groups reciting the rosary to visit seven churches where the Altars of Repose are sumptuously adorned with the most beautiful silver from the treasury of the church; the "tabernacle" is sometimes a beautiful silver box sparkling with brilliant jewels.

In the United States the Altar of Repose is usually decorated with a profusion of the brightest flowers and greens of the season; spotlights and numerous candles illuminate the scene. In the evening a sermon is preached on the Last Supper. The custom, which was common to religious houses, of having voluntary adorers take turns in keeping perpetual day and night watch before the Blessed Sacrament until the removal on the following day, has spread to the churches.

In many countries the silencing of the bells and the use of clappers after the *Gloria* in liturgical ceremonies has produced the popular expression that "the bells have gone to Rome" and will return again after the *Gloria* of Holy Saturday. Children go through the streets sounding various types of rattles and clappers to impress on all the reign of sorrow during these days.

Holy Thursday is called Green Thursday in some countries but there is not agreement as to why this name was chosen. In Austria and Hungary, however, it is the custom to eat spinach and green salad on this day. The reason given is that the Jews ate green vegetables or herbs at their Passover feast.

In Mexico the Indians reenact the Last Supper in their own colorful manner; this is especially elaborate in Tzintzuntzan. The children pretend to drive out devils with their rattles, sometimes dragging an effigy of the Devil through the streets.

Good Friday

It is quite fitting that the "Station Church" for Good Friday should be the Basilica of the Holy Cross in Jerusalem where the relics of the True Cross were received from St. Helena. The sorrow of this day is emphasized by the Church in a somber liturgy. The bishop and his assistants are vested in mournful black as they begin the services prostrate before the altar which is covered with a single cloth. The ceremonies have the ancient form used in those early Christian assemblies on days when Mass was not celebrated. *Lessons* are read from the Old Testament and *Responses*, which call to mind the Passion, are chanted. St. John's Gospel of the Passion is sung by three chanters as on Palm Sunday. A litany of intercessory prayers is then sung by the bishop; it is similar to those preserved from antiquity and used daily in churches of the Eastern Rites.

After the prayers the bishop removes his chasuble and, facing the people from the right of the sanctuary, he unveils the top of the veiled Cross, which he holds in his hand, singing: *"Behold the wood of the Cross."* The ministers continue with him. *"on which hung the salvation of the world."* The choir and clergy kneel and answer: *"Come let us adore."* The bishop ascends to the platform of the altar, uncovers the right arm and the head of the Cross, and in a higher tone the chant is repeated. He then goes to the middle of the altar, uncovers the whole Cross and in a still higher tone sings a third time. He lays the Cross on a cushion; then, removing his shoes, he makes three profound genuflections at short distances from the Cross and reverently kisses the feet of the Crucifix. The triple adoration is performed by the clergy and faithful, while the choir sings the *Reproaches* which begin with the verse: *"O my people, what is it I have done unto thee? How have I grieved thee? Answer thou me."* They are a series of complaints, as it were, of the Saviour. During them is sung, in Greek and Latin, the *Trisagion* of the Greek Liturgy: *"Holy art thou, O God. Holy art thou, O mighty One. Holy art thou O immortal One: Have mercy on us,"* as a sign that the Saviour's sacrifice is the perfect act of worship of the Holy Trinity. Lastly is sung the hymn of the Passion: *"Crux fidelis . . . Faithful cross, amidst all others, Noble tree alone art thou, . . ."*

The Mass of the Presanctified, as it is called, completes the services of Good Friday. The Holy Sacrifice is not offered but there is a Communion Service in which the Host, which was consecrated (hence presanctified) on the previous day and reserved in the Sepulchre, is now consumed. The bishop is led in procession to the Altar of Repose; he kneels in adoration and incenses the Blessed Sacrament. A white veil is draped over his shoulders with which he covers the chalice containing the Host as the solemn procession returns to the altar. The choir sings the famous *Vexilla Regis: "The royal banners now unfurled, the mystic cross illumes the world, . . ."* At the altar the Communion Service consists of the recitation of parts of the daily Mass, ending with the consumption of the Host by the bishop. Although this Mass of the Presanctified seems to have been introduced into the Roman Liturgy as early as the Eighth or Ninth Century, the custom of reserving the Host at the Altar of Repose and of bringing it in procession to the altar developed from the usage of the Papal Court at Avignon in France.

POPULAR CUSTOMS   After Mass on Good Friday the people of Naples carry two statues in procession to the

51

cathedral church where the service of the *Tre Ore* (Three Hours) is to be held. One is the figure of Jesus stretched out in death, the other is the figure of His Mother in sorrow. At dawn the next morning, one procession carries the statue of Jesus in one direction and a second procession carries the statue of the Mother in another; they meet at an appointed spot and the priest preaches a touching sermon on the meeting of Mother and Son as He carried His cross. The children carry the instruments of the Passion in the procession and some of the older ones are clothed in penitential robes and crowns of thorns. On Friday night groups of youth march solemnly through the streets behind a band playing dirges; they stop at intervals and one of the youths preaches on the "Way of the Cross."

The preaching on the Passion of the Three Hours has spread to many countries and is particularly favored in the United States. The large churches are always crowded for this service which is conducted from twelve to three o'clock in the afternoon. Those who cannot find room in the churches hear the services broadcast over loud speakers in the open air or over the radio at home. The sermons are given by eloquent orators on the "Seven Last Words of Our Saviour on the Cross." Between the sermons prayers in common and solemn hymns are sung by select choirs.

In Malta the *Tre Ore* ends dramatically with the lowering of a life-size figure of Our Lord from the Cross. The tremendous procession of the statues and symbols of the Passion then takes place through the streets of the city which are lined with people saying the rosary. Among the representations are: Jesus praying in the garden of olives; Jesus tied to the pillar and scourged; Jesus crowned with thorns; Veronica wiping the face of Jesus;

52

the Sorrowful Mother. The symbols include the crown of thorns, the nails, the garments of Our Lord, and seven banners bearing the Seven Last Words. So anxious are the people to participate in this parade which lasts for hours that they must be chosen according to the alms which they give for charity.

The most elaborate of such processions are probably those of Seville in Spain. They begin on Palm Sunday and are continued on Wednesday, Thursday and Friday of Holy Week. Preceded by the dignitaries of the city and the "Roman Soldiers," the members of Religious Confraternities, clothed in long robes of every color, their heads crowned with long peaked hoods and their hands carrying torches, proceed through the streets. In litters they bear magnificent statues of the Suffering Mother and the most artistic crucifixes of Our Lord. Each representation is a choice treasure which belongs to a particular group or parish.

It is especially in the small towns of Italy and Mexico that the processions have kept the character of a Passion Play. At Sezze, Italy, for example, all the principal characters of the Passion are portrayed and, besides the "Roman Slaves," there are some six hundred "Roman Soldiers" of the imperial era in metal helmets and breastplates. In Mexico the statue of "Jesus in Death" is carried in the procession and is the object of special devotions upon the return to the church.

Austria and Germany have kept the old custom of the Middle Ages when the Sepulchre belonged to Good Friday. A special side chapel is prepared with lamps to which a solemn procession bears the Crucifix. Hymns are sung on the way and then the Crucifix is laid on a pillow for public adoration during the day. In Austria the Sepulchre contains a statue of "Our Lord in Death." There,

53

too, a special Host, which has been consecrated during the Mass of Holy Thursday, is borne in a Monstrance, accompanied by clappers and lights, and exposed for perpetual adoration during the day and night. Soldiers take turns standing at "present arms" during this Eucharistic watch.

Holy Saturday

This is another day of ceremonies rooted in the days of old. Early in the morning on the porch of Rome's Basilica of St. John Lateran, the Cardinal Vicar begins the services with the Blessing of the New Fire. He blesses a small flame, which has been ignited from flint, with prayers that express the spiritual illumination symbolized by new fire. Then he blesses five grains of incense which are to be inserted into the Paschal Candle. The bishop and his attendants enter the basilica behind the deacon who carries aloft a staff capped by a triple candle. The procession halts three times for the lighting of each tip of the candle from the new fire, the deacon singing, *"The Light of Christ,"* and the others answering: *"We thank Thee, O God."*

The inspiring rite of the lighting of the Paschal Candle follows. The deacon ascends the pulpit near which stands the great Paschal Candle. There he sings that ancient song, written in sublime music, which enumerates a long series of the marvelous benefits of God to the human race, calling on all to rejoice, especially in the gift of the Resurrection which is symbolized by the Paschal Candle. This prayer of praise is known as the Easter Laud or the *Exultet* from the opening words: *"Let now in heaven the countless host of Angels hold high festival; with exceed-*

54

ing great joy let the hidden creations of God rejoice; and let the trumpet of salvation sound forth the triumph of the King of Kings. . . ." The song is interrupted at intervals to insert in the Paschal Candle the five grains of incense in the form of a cross and to light the Paschal Candle and the lamps of the sanctuary from the triple candle.

Twelve ancient *Prophecies*, mystically connected with baptism, are then read from the Old Testament; each is followed by a prayer which sums up the thought. At their conclusion a procession wends its way to the ancient baptistery outside the basilica, singing a Psalm that symbolizes the desire for baptism: *"As the hart panteth after the fountains of water; so my soul panteth after thee, O God."* The bishop prays that God may satisfy the holy longings of those "about to be born again."

When all are within the baptistery he sings a beautiful *Preface* extolling the wondrous works which God has wrought through the element of water. At intervals he pauses in the song to divide the water of the font in the form of a cross, to bless it and to sprinkle it to the four points of the compass, a symbol of the river which, issuing from Eden, was divided into four streams to water the earth. As the Holy Spirit once breathed upon the waters of creation, the bishop symbolically breathes upon the water and thrice dips the Paschal Candle into it, singing: *"Upon the plenteous waters of this font may the power of the Holy Spirit come down."* Finally holy chrism is poured into the baptismal water to signify the superabundant grace of baptism. Upon the completion of this blessing of the baptismal water, the procession returns to the basilica singing a litany of invocations.

The Mass which now begins, anticipates the joy of Easter. The opening prayer indicates this spirit in the words: *"O God, who ennoblest this most sacred night with the glory of our Lord's resurrection: foster in the offspring which thou hast but now bestowed upon thine household, the spirit of adoption with which thou hast enriched it.*" So also the *Epistle* urges those risen with Christ to seek the things that are above and the *Gospel* tells the story of the Resurrection. Once more the bells are rung at the *Gloria* and the *Alleluia* which has been suppressed during Lent is sung in special tones. At the end of the Mass it is added to the *Dismissal*.

THE PASCHAL CANDLE   Now that we have seen what happens on Holy Saturday it might make the ceremonies mean more if we recall some of their origins.

We have already narrated what the Pilgrim Etheria described as the rite of the "Illumination" at the beginning of the night vigil in the church of the Resurrection at Jerusalem. Now it seems quite certain that the first part of today's ceremony, the blessing of the new fire and the illumination of the Paschal Candle, is an adaptation of that ancient rite. The rite of the "Illumination" was the lighting of the evening candle at the commencement of the vigil. It was to be placed at the side of the bookstand and consumed in honor of the "Light of Light." In the past the services of Holy Saturday also began with the night vigil, as the prayers which constantly refer to "this night" indicate. That is why they begin now with the blessing of the new fire and the lighting of the Paschal Candle. The prayers and actions as we have seen them are, of course, more elaborate and symbolical than were those of the primitive "Illumination." Now, however, they have lost some of their colorfulness. The singing of the *Exultet*, for example, which was reserved to the deacon, because it was his duty to light the candle at the night watch, used to be read from a parchment scroll which was illustrated with pictures painted upside down so that the people could see them as the scroll unfolded.

THE PROPHECIES   In the early days the neophytes were given their last preparation for baptism on the eve of Easter. They were catechized, exorcised, anointed and then admitted to the church. There they listened to the *Prophecies* read from the Old Testament and joined with the faithful in the chants and prayers between each reading. This was the ancient type of night watch still materially preserved in the liturgy of Holy Saturday.

BAPTISM   The blessing of the baptismal font is a remnant of those days when the Christian neophytes were baptized during the night before Easter. The procession was then an awesome sight as the candidates marched solemnly out under the night skies, their white robes on their arms, to descend to the baptistery where they were to be bathed in the waters of regeneration. Gathered around the bishop, they listened to beautiful prayers for the blessing of the waters and then stepped into the pool where they were immersed under fountains of the life-giving waters. After baptism they were clothed in the white robes and a candle lighted from the Paschal Candle was put into their hands, symbols of the gift they had received. The litany of invocations now sung as the procession returns was originally sung by the faithful and clergy who remained in the church awaiting the return of the newly baptized. The Mass which followed was the Mass of Easter morn, which explains why its theme, as we now have it on Holy Saturday, is that of the Resurrection.

POPULAR CUSTOMS   The "anticipation" of Easter is manifested in a dramatic way in Germany and Austria. In Silesia, during the evening of Holy Saturday, a procession bearing the Blessed Sacraments goes to the Sepulchre. There a statue of the body of Christ is lifted and carried out of the church before the procession. When the procession returns, the statue is placed on the Gospel or right hand side of the main altar, where it remains for the whole week. In the meantime the congregation sings hymns to the resurrected Christ.

In Vienna the procession is a thrilling spectacle. Led by the civil dignitaries to the accompaniment of ringing bells and a band, it is met in the square by a battalion of four thousand men in full dress parade. They stand "at ease" until, at the appearance of the Blessed Sacrament, a trumpet sounds. Then they "present arms," fall upon one knee and salute with white-gloved hands. After the procession has returned to the church, Benediction is held and all sing the *Regina Caeli;* outside the bugle sounds, the soldiers salute and, with band playing, return to their garrison.

In these countries it is also customary to start the Easter Fires on this day. The New Fire for the liturgical ceremonies is sometimes a large fire of logs in front of the cathedral. Children take home part of the burning wood on wires and from these the fire at home is ignited for the cooking of Easter food. On the hills and mountains huge Easter bonfires illuminate the countryside, while flaming hoops of fire are rolled down into the valleys.

In many countries the joy of Easter is dramatically initiated at the *Gloria* of the Mass on Holy Saturday. When the choir starts singing and the bells ringing at the intoning of the *Gloria,* a huge purple curtain which has concealed the altar is drawn aside revealing a spectacle of flowers and candles. In Spain a noise like peals of thunder accompany the bells of the churches. In Florence there is the famous *Scoppio del Carro*—the "explosion of the wagon." At the moment of the *Gloria* a rocket in the shape of a dove is released from high over the main altar of the cathedral; it runs along a wire through the cathedral and out the front door where it lands on a carriage filled with fireworks which are then exploded.

In Italy bands march through the streets after the *Gloria* and children tag along, spinning clackers in their hands. At home the mother of the house goes about striking the doors with a staff to symbolize the expulsion of the devil. The father of the family performs a special blessing at table with the Palm branch of Palm Sunday; special sweet cakes and *pizza* made with eggs are eaten at dinner. The parish priest makes the rounds for the blessing of the houses with holy water. In Germany the holy water is carried home from barrels left outside the churches. The old custom of baptizing on this evening is retained.

Mexico has the colorful ceremony of the "burning of Judas." When all the church bells are ringing at the singing of the *Gloria*, huge paper effigies of Judas, made with a horrible masked face and coins tied to his body which is stuffed with firecrackers, are exploded in mid-air over the principal streets. Smaller ones are set off by the children. Sometimes the effigy is also stuffed with candy which the children rush to gather in when it explodes.

In Poland there is the blessing of the Easter repast by the priest in the homes of the faithful. Everything is laid out in order on tables, sometimes enough for the whole of Easter Week: eggs, of course, artistically decorated, cakes of many sizes, shapes and colors, meats that are

59

the popular favorites, especially hams and sausages, and sweets in the shape of lambs carrying the standard of the Resurrection. These people know how to fast, but they also know how to feast in the spirit of the Church.

Easter Sunday

The "Station" church for Easter Sunday is the Basilica of St. Mary Major. It was chosen because it was near to the Lateran. The people who were weary after the long night services of the vigil, therefore, could get there without too much difficulty. Today, however, the outstanding ceremonies are at St. Peter's. Some seventy thousand people crowd the great basilica at the ten o'clock services to welcome the Pope. The procession to the throne, always magnificent, enters from the Papal Sacristy to the sound of silver trumpets floating down from the balcony. In the long line there are clergy in white surplices, religious in habits of varied color and design, bishops and archbishops in tall white mitres, cardinals in bright red, Noble Guards and Swiss Guards in old world uniforms and finally, borne aloft on a great chair by cerise vested attendants, the Pope crowned with the massive tiara. As they pass down the nave, which is decorated with gold-braided damask drapes and is ablaze with hanging lamps, a roar of welcome rises wave on wave: *"Viva il Papa"*—"Long live the Pope."

The Papal Mass which follows brings forth the full grandeur of the Roman liturgy. The theme of the prayers is the Resurrection, as indicated in the opening words: *"I arose and am still with thee, alleluia."* Between the *Epistle* and *Gospel* is sung the *Easter Sequence*, *"Victimae Paschali"*: *"To the Paschal Victim, hymns of praise come ye Christians joyous raise . . .*" Today the Pope preaches a sermon which is usually a message of world-wide import. After the Mass he proceeds to the great balcony overlooking the vast square in front of the church. There hundreds of thousands kneel to receive the Papal Blessing, called *Urbi et Orbi*, because it is given not only to Rome but to the entire world.

POPULAR CUSTOMS   In Germany after the Gospel of the Resurrection has been read there is a procession through the church with the Blessed Sacrament and a statue of the Resurrection. The statues of the Angels of the Resurrection are placed in the Sepulchre holding a standard on which is inscribed: "Christ is risen."

In Malta a similar procession takes place at dawn. Then a statue of the Resurrected Christ is borne from one church to another.

All Catholic churches are elaborately decorated for Easter with bright lights, candles and spring flowers, especially Easter lilies. Each country has its own favorite Easter hymns which, with the *Alleluia*, tell of the joy of the Resurrection, while the liturgical hymns, such as the *Regina Caeli laetare* (Queen of Heaven rejoice), are universal. Mexico enjoys gay music in the streets, Easter plays and, together with Spain, bull fights. In the United States a milder form of enthusiasm is seen in the gay Easter parades where everyone turns out in new clothes, especially Easter bonnets for the women, to stroll the main thoroughfares and, perhaps, have their photograph taken for the press. In Europe the parading takes the form of hiking on Easter Monday, when people throng the countryside for picnics in the open air or make visits to friends and relatives. In Germany this is

61

called the Emmaus Walk in memory of the two disciples on the road to Emmaus.

It is a universal custom to eat certain foods at Easter time. Spring lamb is popular almost everywhere for the simple reason that it is so intimately connected in symbolism with the "Paschal Lamb." Ham and spiced meats are the usual thing in Europe because they are a stable fare from which the people have abstained during Lent. The eating of eggs on this day is said to have come down from pagan usage of the egg as a symbol of fertility; in Christian adaptation it was made a symbol of the Resurrection since the chicken emerges by itself from the tomb of the eggshell. Some, however, say that eggs were just another of the ordinary foods from which people abstained during Lent and so were abundantly used once the fast was over. At any rate the symbolism is very apt.

It is a common legend in northern European countries that the bells which went to Rome on Holy Thursday bring back the eggs with them when they return on Holy Saturday. In Germany, France and Belgium they are hidden in all sorts of places, especially in the garden, for the children to find in "egg hunts." The "egg races" are competitions in which the young people strive to see who can pick up the most eggs from a long line in a given time without breaking a single one. The rolling of eggs on lawns, a traditional ceremony at the Presidential White House in the United States, is said to symbolize the rolling back of the stone from the sepulchre. Candy and chocolate eggs are a modern invention to please the children, as are the confectioner's Easter bunnies. In some countries the bunny is supposed to lay the eggs because in pagan symbolism the rabbit was a sign of fertility. The painting of Easter eggs is really an art in some of the

62

eastern European countries. The girls of the family spend the long evenings of Lent working with special paints and brushes to execute the intricate and often symbolical designs that ornate these gift eggs of Easter.

5. Pentecost

# 5.	Pentecost

Origin and name

Just as Easter in the beginning was intimately connected with the Jewish feast of the Passover, so Pentecost coincided with another great day in the calendar of the Hebrews. In the Old Testament this day was called the Feast of Weeks because it came just seven weeks after the Passover, that is "on the fiftieth day from the next day after the Sabbath of the Passover." This, of course, would make it on the fiftieth day after our Easter. It was also called the Feast of the Harvest of First Fruits, because it was a festival of thanksgiving for the harvest. For this festival, bread, made from the newly gathered wheat, was offered as a sacrifice. At a later date it was connected with the establishment of the Mosaic Law on Mount Sinai. The name Pentecost was adopted from the Greek-speaking Jews as it was the word for the "fiftieth day" in their language.

It was on this day that the Holy Spirit descended upon the disciples in tongues of fire. This was the coming of the Paraclete, as Our Lord had promised them. With this coming the Apostles were transformed from timid and fearful men into the courageous and dynamic *"ministers of Christ and dispensers of the mysteries of God."* The Church was fully established and set upon its mission of salvation. As St. John Chrysostom says: *"What is there, I ask, which pertains to our salvation, that is not dispensed to us through the Spirit? Through Him we are liberated from slavery, we are called to freedom, we are led to adoption and, finally, I might say, we are molded, putting off the heavy and evil weight of sins. Through the Holy Spirit we behold the choruses of priests and possess the ranks of teachers; from this fountain come the gifts of revelation and the graces of healings; and whatever else adorns the Church of God has there its abundance."*

Mindful of the magnitude of this miraculous event for the Church, the early Christians celebrated this day as a festival of rank similar to that of Easter. Naturally, it was given the same name as the Jewish Feast on which it fell, Pentecost; but the Fathers of the Church emphasized its Christian significance by drawing a comparison between the establishment of the Christian Church and the Mosaic Church which had come into existence on the same day of the year. At first Pentecost was used to signify the whole period of fifty days from Easter to the Descent of the Holy Spirit, although this last day was early celebrated as a special festival. It was a period of continual rejoicing during which no fasting was permitted and prayer was to be made standing without bending the knee. A remnant of this practice continues today in the custom of saying the *Regina Caeli* in a standing position during this time. The Latin Rite did not adopt the name Pentecost until later, when the original Latin name *Quinquagesima* (fiftieth) was in danger of being confused with the pre-Lenten Sunday of Quinquagesima. Our English name of Whitsunday seems to have derived from the white robes that the newly baptized wore on this day.

In Sicily the festival was once known as *Pascha Rosarum* because of the roses that were used in its celebration. Italy called it *Pasqua Rossa* because the vestments worn at Mass were red. The Germans called today

Blumen-Tag (Flower-Day), from the flowers and branches with which they ornamented their houses.

Pentecost in the past

JERUSALEM   The Pilgrim Etheria saw this festival celebrated in Jerusalem as early as the Fourth Century; it was more elaborately observed then than it is now. As at Easter time, the festival began with a vigil, the night watch of prayer and Psalms in the church of the Resurrection, at which the bishop read the Gospel of the Resurrection (as was the custom on every Sunday). At dawn all proceeded to the Holy Sepulchre where they attended Mass and listened to a sermon. About nine o'clock all the people, singing hymns, escorted the bishop to the church at Mt. Sion, where the narrative from the Acts of the Apostles recounting the Descent of the Holy Spirit on the Apostles was read and a second Mass attended. At the *Dismissal*, all were invited to be present in the afternoon for the services on the Mount of Olives. After dinner, everyone in the city ascended to the grotto where Our Lord was accustomed to converse with His disciples. When all were assembled, they proceeded to the site of the Ascension where readings, hymns, prayers and the narratives of the Ascension occupied them until about three o'clock. Descending again to the grotto, the evening prayer service (*Vespers*), beginning with the "Illumination" in the church of the grotto, was conducted; this ended with the blessing of the catechumens and faithful.

As evening approached the multitude slowly wended their way down the mountain singing hymns and Psalms. Night had come when they reached the city gates where they were met by torch bearers and conducted back to the Holy Sepulchre which they reached at eight o'clock. A continual series of prayers and songs at the near-by holy shrines, ending at Mount Sion, kept them occupied until midnight. No wonder the Pilgrim remarked: *"A great labor was borne that day, because from the vigil that began at cockcrow in the church of the Resurrection, there was no letup during the whole day."*

ROME The early Latin liturgy celebrated Pentecost in a manner similar to its Easter ceremonies but on a less elaborate scale. As with every great feast day, so Pentecost had its vigil or night watch. This began at noon on Saturday when the catechumens, who for one reason or another had not been baptized at Easter, were prepared for Baptism and Confirmation on this alternate day. They met in the church, as on Holy Saturday, for the reading of the scriptural *Prophecies* and the prayers in common after each *Prophecy*. Then came the blessing of the baptismal font, followed by the administration of the sacraments, the singing of the *Litanies* and the night Mass of the vigil. In many places, in order to imitate more perfectly the ceremonies of Easter, a rite for the blessing and lighting of a large candle was introduced and was accompanied by a chant like the *Exultet*. In the early days, however, as has been already mentioned, the great candle was lit at the "Illumination" for the beginning of the vigilary office.

On Pentecost Sunday, as at Easter, the newly baptized wore their white robes and went in procession then and during the octave to the "Station Churches." At the Papal Mass in St. Peter's, doves, representing the Holy Spirit, were let loose. Pieces of white wool were thrown down from above to announce the coming of the Holy Spirit. From the round roof of the church, which was once the

70

Pantheon, red roses were floated down like the "tongues of fire." This practice in Sicily caused the feast to be called *Pascha Rosarum*. At one time, in France, trumpets were blown during Mass to signify the roaring of the wind that accompanied the coming of the Holy Spirit.

Pentecost today

When the ancient regulations restricting baptism to Easter and Pentecost were removed, there was no longer need for the long services of the vigil. The services were then advanced to the morning of Saturday, as in the case of Holy Saturday. Now on the Saturday Vigil there remain only vestiges of those early ceremonies and these only at Solemn Mass, at which the six *Prophecies*, the prayers and the *Litanies* are said before the Mass begins. There is still the blessing of the Baptismal Font which must take place in all parish churches on the vigil of Pentecost. The Mass of the Vigil, however, remains much as it was. It begins with the *Gloria*, which was the customary transition from the night office to the Holy Sacrifice of the Mass. (Private Masses have an *Introit*, the usual opening Psalm for Mass.) The first prayer refers to the baptized, begging God, by the illumination of the Holy Spirit, to confirm their hearts; so also does the *Epistle* which narrates the baptism and confirmation of twelve disciples of St. John the Baptist by St. Paul at Ephesus. The *Gospel* and other prayers are concerned with the coming of the Holy Spirit and His works in the souls of men.

The Mass on Pentecost Day is celebrated in the symbolic vestments of red and is a glorious drama when en-

71

acted in its full liturgical scene of clergy, decoration and specially arranged chant. Everything brings home to the faithful the grandeur of the event celebrated. The opening Psalm (*Introit*) sings: "*The Spirit of the Lord hath filled the whole earth, Alleluia; and that which containeth all things hath knowledge of the voice, Alleluia, Alleluia, Alleluia.*" The first prayer is a favorite of the people: "*O God, who on this day didst instruct the hearts of the faithful by the light of the Holy Spirit; grant that by the same Spirit we may relish what is right, and ever rejoice in His consolation.*" The *Epistle,* from the Acts of the Apostles, recounts again, as it did in the time of the Pilgrim, the story of the descent of the Holy Spirit in tongues of fire upon the disciples. Then comes the beautiful hymn attributed to Innocent III, *Veni Sancte Spiritus* (Come Holy Spirit), which is at once a prayer of praise and petition. The *Gospel* gives the consoling message which Our Lord addressed to the Apostles as He took farewell of them at the Last Supper; though He must leave them, He would abide in them and send the Holy Spirit to comfort them and teach them all truth. The other special prayers of the Mass dwell harmoniously on the same theme of the coming and consolation of the Holy Spirit.

After Mass on the Saturday following Pentecost the Easter Cycle or Paschal Season comes to an end. Trinity Sunday follows and from then until the Christmas Cycle, which begins with the first Sunday of Advent, the Sundays are numbered according to their sequence after Pentecost. There cannot be fewer than twenty-three or more than twenty-eight until Advent. This period represents the workings of the Holy Spirit in the hearts of men until the end of time.

A Portuguese custom

The Portuguese have a very special devotion to the Holy Spirit which is said to date back to the time of St. Elizabeth, Queen of Portugal, in the Fourteenth Century. The tale relates that she was privately inspired to build a church in honor of the Holy Spirit and that after it was completed she held a great feast for all the workmen and for the poor. This charity to the poor was annually repeated by the nobles until it became a universal custom with a ritual of its own. The Portuguese people have carried it with them to their homes in the Azores and in America. On Pentecost Sunday, and in the Azores for the seven Sundays after Easter, the people hold a procession with flowers, banners and songs, led by one who has been chosen as the "Emperor." They enter the church and attend Mass, after which the priest blesses and crowns the "Emperor." The crown, which has been placed on the altar and surrounded with flowers and candles during the Mass, is a beautiful silver piece of open work with four arcs, mounted by a cross and a dove. The procession then marches to the home of the "Emperor" who furnishes a fine feast, especially for the poor, while speeches and songs entertain the guests. The "Emperor" is allowed to keep the crown until another has been elected. This is a great honor for behind it is the significance of the spirit of charity that is poured forth by the Holy Spirit into the hearts of the faithful.

The dove

The dove is the symbol of the Holy Spirit and in Austria and Germany it is still customary to have a painted wooden dove suspended over the altar at the Mass on Pentecost. At Orvieto, in Italy, there is a special celebration in the evening, representing the descent of the Holy Spirit. The townsfolk gather in the great square before the cathedral, which is decorated with flowers and lights. Music is played and songs are sung until the spectacular moment when the dove, with outstretched wings, is run along a wire to descend on the scene of the Apostles who are gathered together in the Supper Room, which has been reconstructed on a platform before the doors of the cathedral.

6.   Corpus Christi

6. Corpus Christi

Origin of the festival

Mention has already been made of the fact that in the ancient liturgy of the Church Holy Thursday was especially devoted to the memory of the institution of the Blessed Sacrament and for that reason was called The Mystic Supper, The Birthday of the Eucharist, The Birthday of the Chalice, or The Day of the Mysteries. In those days three Masses were celebrated on this Thursday, one for the penitents who were to be publicly reconciled, one for the blessing of oils to be used in Baptism and Extreme Unction, and the last, in the evening, for the commemoration of the Last Supper and the Easter Communion. In time, however, circumstances changed, the three Masses became one and more and more emphasis was put on the sorrowful mysteries of Holy Week. As a result the special commemoration intended on this day was obscured. The Church early recognized this tendency. Many centuries before the institution of the present festival it concentrated the thoughts of the faithful on the Holy Eucharist in the Mass of Wednesday which follows immediately after Pentecost; in it the *Introit* and the *Gospel* refer especially to the Eucharistic Bread of Life. Nevertheless, this was not sufficient to attain the special and solemn remembrance desired and subsequent heresies regarding the Eucharist provided another motive for the institution of a separate festival.

An added impetus was given by the events that had taken place in Belgium at Liége.

In the thirteenth century in a convent of Augustinian nuns at Mont Cornillon, near Liége, there lived a holy religious called Juliana of Retinnes (Retinnes being the town of her birth). This young girl had a very tender devotion to the Blessed Sacrament and during her prayers was granted a vision of the moon in splendor but with part of its sphere broken away. Imploring God's help to understand its meaning, it was revealed to her that the moon represented the Church, but the break indicated the lack of a solemnity in honor of the Eucharist. It seems that for many years Juliana kept this secret to herself, confiding only in her friend Eve, a recluse of the city. Some years later when she was elected prioress of the house at Mont Cornillon she communicated her revelations to John of Lausanne, a Canon of the basilica of St. Martin. He was immediately moved to promote the adoption of a special festival, but prudently decided that the whole matter should receive the approval of learned men. In this way he gained support for the cause which was of great importance in the eyes of the Church, for not only did the theologians of the Dominican Order put their stamp of approval on the doctrine contained in this subject, but such men as Hugh of Saint-Cher, the Provincial of the Dominicans and Philip, Chancellor of the University of Paris, added prestige to the movement. From other groups of clerics and people, however, came strong opposition, some even persecuting Juliana. Finally, the bishop of Liége, Robert of Torote, investigated the dispute and vindicated Juliana and Eve. James Pantaleon of Troyes, the Archdeacon of Liége, also gave his approval which was of great importance, because he was ultimately to be the Pope to establish the festival. Bishop Robert then decreed that the feast be celebrated by the Canons of Saint Martin's, but he died before witnessing the cele-

78

bration which Eve persuaded the Canons to carry out against all opposition.

Four years later, in 1252, Hugh the Dominican, who had now become the Cardinal Legate, returned to Liége and gave his approval to the festival which he himself celebrated. He then spread its observance into the four countries of his jurisdiction. Juliana died in exile at Fosses in 1258, but Eve carried on the work of promoting the festival by writing of the life of Juliana and her revelations. At her instigation the bishop of Liége wrote to Urban IV in 1261 requesting him to make the feast universal. The Pope replied favorably and three years later sent to all bishops the Bull "*Transiturus*" (September 8, 1264), directing that the universal celebration of a festival in honor of the Blessed Sacrament be held on the Thursday after Trinity Sunday.

It seemed that the long struggle of Juliana and Eve had come to an end and that all the world would now acknowledge the new festival. However, there was still a long delay. This was caused by the death of Urban IV shortly after the promulgation of the Bull, the absence from Rome of the succeeding Popes because of the troubled times, and the consequent disruption of unified observances in the liturgy. At the Ecumenical Council of Vienne in 1311, however, Pope Clement V renewed the decree of Urban IV in a new Bull so that, little by little, the festival began to be observed in more places until it was well established in the Fourteenth Century.

The Mass

St. Thomas Aquinas, the "Angelic Doctor" of theology, who is reported to have said that his greatest knowledge was gained in the presence of the Blessed Sacrament, was commissioned to write the Office and Mass for this festival. His work is a testimony to his own devotion, for it is admitted by all to be among the most beautiful in the Roman liturgy. The opening Psalm in the *Introit* of the Mass shouts aloud the joy of the Church for the gift of the Sacrament: *"He fed them with the fat of wheat, alleluia; and filled them with honey out of the rock, alleluia, alleluia, alleluia. Rejoice to God our helper; sing aloud to the God of Jacob."* The *Prayer* recalls to us the connection of this Sacrament with the redemptive work of the Passion: *"O God, who in this wonderful sacrament hast left us a memorial of thy passion: grant us, we beseech thee, so to reverence the sacred mysteries of thy body and blood, that we may ever feel within us the fruit of thy redemption."* The *Epistle*, which is taken from St. Paul's words to the Corinthians, recalls the institution of the Holy Eucharist at the Last Supper and again stresses its relation to the Passion: *"For as often as you shall eat this bread, and drink this chalice, you shall show the death of the Lord until he come."* It concludes with a warning to prove one's self, by the removal of sin before receiving this Sacrament.

Between the *Epistle* and the *Gospel* is chanted the famous *Lauda Sion*, the hymn in which St. Thomas combines majestic meter, ecstatic praise, and profound doctrine. No translation conveys the beauty of the original Latin, but a short citation may indicate something of its theme:

80

Praise thou, Sion, praise thy Saviour
Praise thy prince with all thy fervour!
Anthems to thy shepherd sing.

All thou canst do thou endeavor,
Yet thy praise can equal never
Such as merits thy great king.

Christian truth uncontroverted
Is that bread and wine converted
Sacred flesh and blood become.

Flesh and blood, our life sustaining,
Christ intact in both remaining,
'Neath each sign we greet.

The *Gospel* of the Mass contains Our Lord's words to the multitudes after the miracle of the multiplication of the loaves and fishes. There is the promise of a bread much greater than that with which the people have just been miraculously fed, much more lasting than the manna of the desert, because it is the bread of eternal life, His own Body and Blood that He will one day give them. The remaining prayers that are proper to this Mass re-echo the blessings of the Eucharist.

The procession

Externally, the distinguishing feature of this festival is the solemn procession of the Blessed Sacrament. This was not an original part of the ceremonies on this day but something that developed in time. It was not an entirely new practice, for even before the establishment of this

81

feast day there were local processions with the Blessed Sacrament at certain times of the year. Thus in Eleventh Century England the Sacred Host was carried outside the church in procession on Palm Sunday. Then there were the processions inside the church during Holy Week—as has already been mentioned. In those days, however, the Sacred Host was hidden from the eye, enclosed in reliquaries of various types or in the chalice. What was new in the Corpus Christi procession was the public veneration of the Blessed Sacrament which was exposed to view for that single purpose. It seems to have developed naturally from the devotion of the faithful on this day. Germany and France began the practice towards the end of the Thirteenth Century and the early part of the Fourteenth in the cities of Cologne, Würtzburg, Augsburg, Chartres, Paris, Sens and Aix-la-Chapelle. It spread more rapidly to other countries after Popes Martin V and Eugene IV granted indulgences to those who took part in the procession in the Fifteenth Century.

Today the grandeur of the procession varies in different localities, but its liturgy is the same everywhere. At the end of the Mass the celebrant is vested in a cope and a veil is put around his shoulders; with the ends of this he holds the monstrance (a tall silver or gold vessel for holding the circular crystal in which the Blessed Sacrament is exposed) and faces the people. The procession then forms behind the white standard of the Holy Eucharist: the children, the confraternities of the parish, the choir, and the clerics proceed in order, each group behind its proper standard or a cross. The celebrant carries the Blessed Sacrament under a canopy, surrounded by his assistants and the incense and torch bearers. As the procession begins, the people fall in at the rear and everyone sings hymns taken from the office of the day. Along the way there are

82

sometimes temporary altars constructed, at some of which a halt is made and the blessing given with the Sacrament. Upon returning to the church there is a final benediction at the main altar.

Medieval pageantry

In the Middle Ages all Europe was Catholic and the festival celebrations of the Church were a matter of truly public observance by whole countries. As the Corpus Christi procession became a widespread custom, it also became a great public pageant. From all ranks of society representative groups were allowed to take an active part in the great processions that passed through the streets of the cities. Kings and emperors, royalty and public officials, regiments of military and confraternities of the faithful all had their place, along with the various ranks of the clergy. All the splendor that could come from palace and state were added to the beauty of the liturgy.

The Church had long been the sponsor of the principal drama of those days, which was Biblical, and this was soon joined to the celebration of the festival. Especially in England, but also in Spain, Italy and Germany, the development of the "Mystery Plays" was connected with the procession of Corpus Christi. At first the plays entered the procession as simple tableaux of some scene from the Bible connected with the glorification of the Blessed Sacrament. Gradually, however, these became little dramas which were enacted on platforms carried along on men's shoulders during the procession. It was considered a great honor to take part in these plays and the expenses for their production was paid by the citizens. Many Corpus Christi Guilds numbering thousands

83

of members were organized and arranged for the production of these plays.

Modern survival

The changing circumstances recorded in history have altered most of that ancient pageantry, but the procession of Corpus Christi is still a spectacle of beauty. Even in countries where it is limited to the precincts of the parish church, it is produced with richly ornamented vestments, bright banners, lights, little girls in white dresses and veils scattering flowers in the pathway, and altar boys in white surplices and various colored cassocks, all singing the age-old hymns.

"Infiorata" at Genzano

In nations where the procession still passes through the public streets, much of the old grandeur remains. The towns and cities of Italy are decorated in festive array. From the windows of the houses are hung long oblong cloths of various bright colors. Across the streets are stretched arches of green branches and flowers, from which lanterns are suspended. So beautiful and artistic is the display at Genzano it has been given the title of *"Infiorata."* From a central square the long wide Via Livia mounts up to the very steps of the church of St. Mary of the Summit. Along this street, from side to side, are strewn thousands of flowers for the Corpus Christi procession. The flowers are arranged in great squares and woven into intricate designs so as to form huge pictures, like mosaics, which often portray some great event of the year. Noted artists make the plans for the panels and skilled workmen produce the scene. The great procession takes place in the evening when the Blessed Sacrament is carried by the ecclesiastical dignitaries over the magnificent tapestry of flowers and up the flight of stairs to the church on the summit.

Austria and Germany

Before the war Germany and Austria were famous for their Corpus Christi processions. It was the custom in Germany for the local parishes to have their own procession on the Thursday of the festival, then, on the following Sunday all the parishes of the city met at the cathedral for a tremendous procession through the streets of the city. All along the pathway of the procession the houses were decorated with streamers and flowers and especially with the bright green branches of young birches. In the doorways or windows miniature altars were set up and adorned. In the fields of the farmlands four separate altars were arranged by different groups of volunteers. They were beautifully decorated and the ground before them was covered with bright flowers set in an artistic design. There the procession halted to sing parts of the Four Gospels, then followed invocations for good crops, suitable weather and freedom from calamities. The fields and people were blessed with the Blessed Sacrament and the procession returned to the church for Benediction and the singing of the Te Deum. The ordinary processions were elaborate enough with their church flags, bands and colorful costumes, but in Austria, Vienna beheld several regiments of soldiers parading in their finest and, in the old days, even the Emperor joined the procession.

85

Seville, Dance of the Seises

Seville in Spain retains an ancient and unique custom on the occasion of this festival. It is called the Dance of the Seises and takes place in the great cathedral. In the evening, after the singing of the Office, there is a procession from the choir to the chancel. When everyone has reached his appointed place, twelve little boys advance before the high altar. They are dressed in medieval costumes of blue and white silk jackets and breeches, white silk stockings and buckled shoes. Large brimmed hats decorated with long feathers complete their attire. To the accompaniment of soft music and the clicking of castanets, these little pages perform a stately and solemn minuet, before the Blessed Sacrament; like David before the Ark, they sing hymns of praise in old religious hymns.

Anniversary at Liége

Liége in Belgium conducted a magnificent celebration for two weeks in 1946 to commemorate the Seventh Century of its Corpus Christi festival. The diocese spent almost two years in preparation for the *Fête-Dieu* (Festival of God), as this feast is beautifully called by the French-speaking nations. The basilica of St. Martin, where the feast was born, dominated the festivities from the hilltop on which it stands. At night it shone forth in massive splendor, illuminated by great searchlights. To it came the pilgrims for the special indulgence granted during the celebration. On the first day fifty thousand children mounted to its heights after participating at solemn Masses held for them throughout the city.

Each successive day found groups of the diocese taking

their turn at services conducted for them in the basilica. On the night of the vigil, the Dominicans chanted the Office which had been composed by their sainted brother Thomas of Aquinas seven centuries before.

An Evening Mass for the workers was attended by some twenty thousand in the stadium. Each group of young workers was represented by a symbolic participation in the Mass. The altar represented the toil of the carpenters and machinists; the white altar linen that of the young seamstresses; the miners in work clothes brought their little lights to illuminate the candles; fathers of families brought bread; mothers brought wine; a goldsmith brought the delicately wrought chalice; a young priest accompanied by his working class parents brought the altar stone; bookmakers the missal, embroiderers the vestments, flower merchants the flowers and, in a touching scene, the mutilated victims of labor and war carried the crucifix. It was their Mass and they all shared in it.

Perhaps the most magnificent spectacle was the procession on the river Meuse which flows through the center of the city. A huge flotilla of boats was drawn down the center of the river whose banks were lined with hundreds of thousands of the faithful. Led by the processional cross on the prow of the first boat, a long series of beautifully decorated floats followed. Before the eyes of the reverent spectators passed living tableaux of the great religious origins of the city, its early saints and medieval village. Then came the pictured story of the great events in the life of St. Juliana in her long struggle to establish the feast. Afterward, as represented in the floats of different cities of Belgium and the floats of the arts and industries, there appeared the modern era of devotion to the Eucharist. The people knelt in silence as the last two boats passed by, that of the Blessed Virgin and that of the Blessed Sacrament held by the bishop surrounded by the first communicants. As the floating choir sang the sacred hymns, airplanes swooped low dropping flower petals over the river. The final benediction was given from a high terrace looking down on the immense throng of boats and canoes that had massed with the flotilla on the river.

On two other days there were processions, reminiscent of those of the Middle Ages, through the streets decorated with flowers and banners. In these the whole history of the Eucharist was represented, its prefigurations in the Old Testament, its institution in the New Testament and the establishment of the feast. In the miles-long procession all the Eucharistic associations and Catholic Action groups marched with their bright colored banners. A full description of these processions and of the other inspiring events of the celebration would fill many a page, but these few words give some idea of the grandeur of it all.

Miraculous Corporal of Orvieto

The Holy Year of 1950 witnessed an extraordinary event in the Corpus Christi procession at St. Peter's in Rome. It was the presence in the procession of the "Miraculous Corporal" of Orvieto. Through the centuries the story of this sacred relic has come down to us by popular tradition. It tells us that in the year 1263 or 1264 a certain priest from Bohemia, called Peter of Prague, was making a pilgrimage to Rome that he might pray before the tombs of the Apostles and be freed from doubts that had long tormented him regarding the Real Presence of Our Lord in the Holy Eucharist. On his way he stopped in the little village of Bolsena where he went to the church of

St. Christina to celebrate Mass. At the moment of the breaking of the Host before the *Communion*, he beheld to his amazement blood gushing forth and falling on the corporal. Fearful and bewildered, he enclosed the Host in the white linen and fled to the sacristy. Pope Urban IV, then visiting at near-by Orvieto, was informed of the matter and sent the bishop of that town to investigate and bring back the relic. The Pope himself went with his court to meet the returning prelate bearing the corporal which was deposited in a sacred place. Presumably this incident influenced the Pope in issuing the Bull of 1264 establishing the feast of Corpus Christi. In 1337 the Sienese artist, Ugolino di Maestro Vieri, made a beautiful silver reliquary, studded with gems and adorned with enamellings that portray the miracle. This was placed in the chapel "of the Corporal" in the famous cathedral of Orvieto which was begun in 1285; the walls are charmingly decorated with frescoes by Ugolino di Prete Ilario depicting the miraculous events.

Through the initiative of Monsignor Francesco Pieri, Bishop of Orvieto, this storied relic was transported outside its town for the first time in over six hundred years and carried in procession to the city of the Popes. The Corpus Christi procession at St. Peter's in Rome is always colorful but this Holy Year procession included not only the long lines of Papal Gendarmes, Palatine Guards, religious orders, canons regular, clergy, students etc., but the Pope Himself was borne under the colonnade and out into the square, kneeling before the Blessed Sacrament which was fixed in a mounted ostensorium. The Papal Court of Swiss Guards, monsignori, bishops and cardinals accompanied the Pope, while immediately before them the reliquary of the "Miraculous Corporal" was carried by special attendants and four valets in medieval costume.

At the finish of the procession the relic was placed above a great altar which had been erected before the central doors of St. Peter's and the Pope gave the benediction with the Blessed Sacrament. The return of the holy relic to Orvieto was a triumphal procession through the small villages north of Rome. In each of the principal villages, which were decorated with flowers and green branches, the cortege paused for a short time to allow the people to manifest their veneration.

7. *The "crown" worn by the "emperor" in the Portuguese ceremony (Pentecost)*

*Casting flowers on the waters
in memory of those lost at sea (Corpus Christi
at Gloucester)*

9. *Laying the flower designs for the*
Corpus Christi procession at Genzano di Roma, Italy

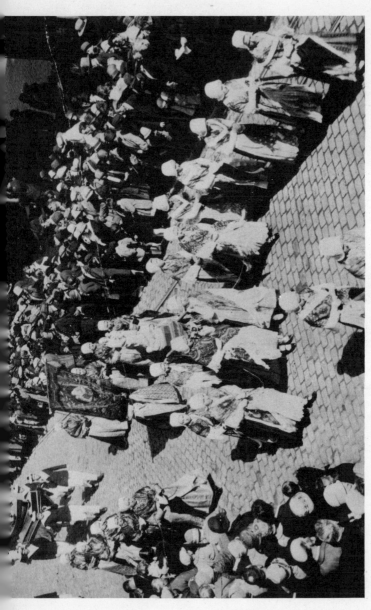

10.　*Fisher-maids in the procession of "Our Lady of Boulogne" (The Assumption)*

7. The Assumption of the Blessed Virgin Mary

7. The Assumption of the Blessed Virgin Mary

Festivals of Our Lady

From its very early days the Church has venerated Our Lady in a special way. We find evidence of this in the writings of the men who lived in the period immediately following that of the Apostles, thus indicating that the devotion was of Apostolic origin. Somewhat later the inscriptions, paintings and welded glass iconography of the Catacombs manifest this devotion among the early Christians. Long before there were definite feast days dedicated to her honor, there were churches, both in the East and the West, erected to her memory. The various feast days that commemorate Our Lady's titles and privileges developed in time.

In the beginning she was implicitly commemorated in those feast days of Our Lord that celebrated events in His life with which she was intimately connected and the ancient sermons preached on those days portray her participation. Gradually the features which especially concerned Our Lady were set apart and made into festivals reserved to her honor. Although these festivals were not very numerous in the infant liturgy, they multiplied very rapidly with the development of Marian theology and with the miracles, apparitions and favors attendant on devotion to the Blessed Virgin. Today the Universal Church observes *seventeen festivals in her honor*. The number celebrated in particular countries and certain localities, however, is even greater than this. A general consideration of this vast array would be inept, so our attention must be given to one of them, the one that is the crown of them all—the Assumption.

The Holy Year definition

It is particularly suitable at this time to consider the festival of the Assumption because of its recent exaltation. For many years the whole Catholic world had offered up prayers and petitions for the authoritative declaration of the belief of the ages in the Assumption of Our Blessed Lady into heaven. After long and careful consideration of the foundations for this belief and the reasons for publicly glorifying it, Pope Pius XII answered the requests of the faithful. In a Papal Bull, *"Munificentissimus Deus,"* issued on November 1, in the Holy Year of 1950, he defined *"that it is a divinely revealed dogma that the Immaculate Mother of God, ever Virgin Mary, when the course of her earthly life was finished, was taken up body and soul into heavenly glory."*

The importance of this great proclamation was attested to by the magnificent ceremonies attendant upon the historic event. On the afternoon previous to the day of definition, the venerable Image of the Blessed Virgin (taken from the Basilica of St. Mary Major, the *"Salus Populi Romani"* or "Health of the People of Rome") was borne in an immense procession from the church of Santa Maria in Ara Coeli, on the Capitoline Hill, to the Square of St. Peter. The great flight of steps leading to Santa Maria was a pathway of colored banners and standards matched in brilliance by the drapes from the balconies of the palaces on the Capitoline. The Image of the Virgin, mounted on a golden throne and carried on the shoulders of the Franciscan Friars of the adjacent monastery, evoked the cry of *"Viva Maria"* from the vast throng below in the Square of Ara Coeli. Accompanied by the presiding bishop, cardinals, civic representatives, selected church organizations and thousands of pilgrims, the Image was borne through streets which were decorated with festive lights and from whose colorfully-draped balconies flowers floated down on the procession. When St. Peter's Square was reached, the Image was placed on high before the central entrance to the basilica and the immense throng sang the *Salve Regina*. Over the broadcasting system came the voice of the Holy Father reciting from his chapel a special prayer to Mary which he had composed for the occasion. At its conclusion he appeared at a window of the Vatican to bestow on all his blessing.

The next morning at 8:30 the ceremonies for the Solemn Definition began at St. Peter's. From the bronze doors of the Vatican there issued a great procession led by the clerics of the Mendicant Orders and followed by the Monastic Orders, the Canon Regulars and the secular clergy. Then came the Papal cortege of Swiss Guards and members of the Papal Court, the bishops and archbishops numbering over 600, the Patriarchs, 36 cardinals and groups of officials. The procession had lasted an hour when the Pope appeared, borne on the *Sedia Gestatoria*. The great crowd which had been gathering since the early hours of the morning and numbered close to 400,000, roared its acclamations: *"Viva Il Papa,"* and for the occasion, *"Viva L'Assunta."* Sitting on a throne which had been erected before the basilica and beneath the Image of Mary, the Holy Father received the obediences of the Cardinal-Bishops. An official request was then made for the Definition, to which the Pope replied briefly and intoned the *Veni Creator*. Before the silent

95

thousands he read the essential parts of the Definition. When it was finished happy cheers filled the air and the artillery batteries on the Janiculum thundered forth in salute. The Pope preached a short sermon and the Papal Mass followed in the basilica.

From ancient times

As the Holy Father stated in the Dogmatic Bull, the festival of the Assumption was celebrated in the Church from ancient times. We do not know the exact date or place of its origin, but some have thought that it arose from a traditional shrine in Jerusalem. This was called the *Dormitio* (Falling Asleep) and was a chapel in the northwest corner of a Byzantine Church called Holy Sion. This church included the Cenacle (Room of the Last Supper) and the *Dormitio* which, according to an old tradition, was the place of Mary's death. The church, destroyed by the Moslems in the Tenth Century and rebuilt by the Crusaders, was again destroyed. Only the Cenacle was left standing.

Towards the end of the Fourth Century there was a festival of Our Lady celebrated at Antioch under the title, "The Memory of the Holy and Ever Virgin Mary, Mother of God." This may be the first trace of our festival, because when days were established in memory of the saints, the day chosen was their "Birthday," that is the day of their entrance into heaven. It is in the Fifth Century, however, that mention is made in Syria of the festival of the Assumption. In Jerusalem around the beginning of the Sixth Century it was already an annual feast. It was in the same century that the Byzantine Emperor, Maurice, decreed that it should always be celebrated

96

thereafter in the Empire on August 15th. St. Gregory of Tours informs us that this festival was celebrated in the Sixth Century in France during January. Rome seems to have instituted the feast in imitation of the Orient. Just when this was done we do not know, but it was so well established there in the Seventh Century that Pope Sergius I decreed that on this day there should be conducted a solemn procession from the church of St. Adrian to the Basilica of St. Mary Major.

Rome also took the Greek name of the festival, *koimesis* (Falling Asleep), which commemorated not only Mary's death, but also her Assumption. In the early days it was also called The Passing, The Deposition and The Repose of Our Lady. Gradually, however, the name Assumption supplanted all other names since it indicated so well the great privilege commemorated in the festival, the entrance into heaven of the body and soul of the Mother of God.

The procession in the Middle Ages

From the description of the ceremonies as they were conducted in the Twelfth Century we learn that on the morning of the Vigil of the Assumption the Pope and the cardinals went barefooted to unveil the Image of the Saviour, an ancient picture supposed to have been miraculously painted and which was preserved at the Lateran. They made seven genuflections before kissing the feet of the Image and then sang the Te Deum. That evening the Pope attended the Office of the Vigil at St. Mary Major. When this was over he returned to St. John Lateran where the people awaited him. From the basilica came the cardinals and deacons bearing the Image of the Sav-

97

iour. A procession formed behind them headed by the Cross bearer, then the members of the Papal Court, the School of Singers and, finally, all the people. Surrounded with torch bearers, the Holy Image was borne through the illuminated streets to the church in the Forum called Santa Maria Nuova. There a ceremony of washing the feet of the Image with aromatic water was performed. While the School of Singers sang the Office of *Matins* in the church, the people, singing hymns, carried the Image to the church of St. Adrian for a second washing of the feet. The procession then returned and climbed the Esquiline Hill to St. Mary Major, where the *Litanies* were finished and the Pope said Mass and blessed the weary multitude. The Image of Mary, the *Salus Populi Romani*, was kept at St. Mary Major and this procession with the Image of the Saviour to her temple seems to have signified the glorious meeting of Mother and Son which was effected by the Assumption.

The Mass of the Assumption

The Rev. Alban Butler in his *Lives of the Saints* beautifully expresses the spirit of the Mass of the Assumption when he writes:

"*The Assumption of the Virgin Mary is the greatest of all the festivals which the church celebrates in her honour. It is the Consummation of all the other great mysteries by which her life was rendered most wonderful; it is the birthday of her true greatness and glory, and the crowning of all the virtues of her whole life, which we admire single in her other festivals. It is for all these gifts conferred on her that we are on this day to praise and thank him who is the author of them; but especially for that glory with which he hath crowned her. In this we must join our homages and joy with all the blessed spirits in heaven."*

So it is that the Church begins the Mass by summoning all to join in this spirit: *"A great sign appeared in heaven: a woman clothed with the sun, and the moon was under her feet, and upon her head a crown of twelve stars* (Apoc. 12, 1). *Sing to the Lord a new song, because he has done wonderful things.* (Ps. 97, 1).

At the *Collect*, are said the words: *Almighty God of eternal life by whom Mary, the immaculate Virgin Mother of thy Son, was assumed into the glory of heaven in body and soul, grant, we beseech thee, that by keeping our minds ever fixed on heavenly things we may become worthy to share her glory."*

The *Epistle* of the Mass is taken from the Book of Judith (13, 22-25; 15, 10) and, as it is often done in the liturgy, the words of the Old Testament are applied by a comparison to Our Lady: *"The Lord hath blessed thee by his power, because by thee he hath brought our enemies to naught. Blessed art thou, O daughter, by the Lord the most high God, above all women upon the earth. Blessed be the Lord, who made heaven and earth, who hath directed thee to cutting off the head of the prince of our enemies; because he hath so magnified thy name this day, that thy praise shall not depart out of the mouth of men, who shall be mindful of the power of the Lord forever, for that thou hast not spared thy life, by reason of the distress and tribulation of thy people, but hast prevented our ruin in the presence of our God. Thou art the glory of Jerusalem, thou art the joy of Israel, thou art the honour of our people."*

The *Gospel* from St. Luke (1, 41-50) tells of the visit

of Mary to her cousin Elizabeth: *"At that time: Elizabeth was filled with the Holy Spirit, and cried out with a loud voice, saying, 'Blessed art thou among women and blessed is the fruit of thy womb! And how have I deserved that the mother of my Lord should come to me? For behold, the moment that the sound of thy greeting came to my ears, the babe in my womb leapt for joy. And blessed is she who has believed, because the things promised her by the Lord shall be accomplished.' And Mary said: 'My soul magnifies the Lord, and my spirit rejoices in God my Saviour; because he has regarded the lowliness of his handmaid; for behold, henceforth all generations shall call me blessed; because he who is mighty has done great things for me, and holy is his name; and for generation upon generation is his mercy, to those who fear him.'"*

Processions

Many European countries and South American nations have retained the ancient custom of holding processions on this day. In France this is a tradition from the days when King Louis XIII dedicated the kingdom to the Blessed Virgin, decreeing that this festival should be celebrated throughout the realm with great solemnity. In 1922 Pope Pius XI confirmed the choice of the Blessed Virgin, as the principal patron of France, under the title of the Assumption, together with all the honors and privileges belonging to this dedication. It is particularly in the small towns, such as Folgoet, that these processions are most colorful. The people appear for the festival in the age old costumes of bright colors and intricate design that are peculiar to their province. After the Mass the statue of Our Lady is carried in procession around the church.

Then the people sit down to enjoy lunch outdoors and the entertainments of a small scale fair.

From ancient times, the festival of the Assumption was reserved for the blessing of plants, probably, according to early writers, to counteract a pagan custom. In Austria it is popularly called The Blessing of Herbs. The procession for this ceremony is practically the same as that on Corpus Christi. The statue of Our Lady is borne on a litter and the priest follows with the Blessed Sacrament. In the fields where four altars have been set up, parts of the Four Gospels are read and prayers are said for good weather and good crops; then the blessing is given with the Blessed Sacrament.

The "Palio of Sienna"

One of the most famous celebrations, from medieval times, in honor of Our Lady's Assumption is the *Palio* (Standard), held at Sienna. The city is divided into wards, each having its own banner which is kept in a parish church. In honor of the Virgin, each ward sends a horse to race in the public square for the prize *Palio*. In the afternoon the horse is brought to the church to be blessed. Then each group with its horse wends its way through the narrow streets to the great square before the cathedral where all gather to receive the best wishes of the bishop. Descending through the crowd-lined street which is decorated with flags and banners, they come to the public square before the city hall. Dressed in the picturesque costumes of the Middle Ages, a great procession passes around the racetrack in review. Announced by the herald who is followed by the mace bearers and trumpeters, come the various representatives of the governing powers of the wards, the drummer, the standard bearer, the captain, the pages and the grooms, the men at arms, and the triumphal-car bearing the *Palio*. The race itself takes place when everyone has been settled into the viewing stands. Twice around the track go the bareback riders in a short but furious scramble, for the corners are square and many a rider lands against their padded sides before the race is finished. To the winner goes the *Palio* and to his ward a happy celebration.

The Mystery of Elche

In southern Spain, in the little Moorish town of Elche on the Mediterranean, it has been the custom from about the Fourteenth Century to celebrate the festival of the Assumption with a "mystery play." It is more of an operetta than a play for the words are sung in a sort of semi-plain chant. An old legend says that the statue of Our Lady of the Assumption and the first manuscript of the play were found in a box on the seashore. On two successive days, the Vigil and the Feast, the "mystery" is performed in the cathedral which has been set up like a theatre, after first removing the sacred things. On the afternoon of the Vigil the drama of the Virgin's Death takes place. "Mary" enters the church with a little group representing other Marys and angels; she passes up the main aisle of the crowded church to the stage which has been erected under the dome. The play begins with "Mary" singing a song expressing a desire to leave this world. The song carries on with variations until the Virgin kneels at the side of her bed. Then a large round sphere which represents heaven is lowered from the dome; it unfolds like a flower and an angel steps forth with a palm branch which he presents to the Virgin and announces her approaching death. He departs again in the golden ball. The next scene shows the Apostles arriving and attending the death bed of the Virgin. The heavens open again and a golden pedestal, called the Ara Coeli, descends with the angel of death and angel musicians who are to bear the soul of Mary, represented by a small image, back to heaven.

On the day of the festival, after a procession with the statue of the Assumption, the play is resumed with the "burial of the Virgin." Then follow the dramatic moment when the Ara Coeli descends again from the heavens and the angel steps forth to reenact again the raising of Mary from the tomb, her crowning and her ascent in the Ara Coeli to heaven. In its setting of colorful costumes, enchanting music and song, this "mystery" has kept the enthusiasm of the people through the ages.

Illustrations Acknowledgments

1. *Courtesy of the Jesuit Missions*

3. *Courtesy of the* Boston Herald

6. *Courtesy of Nora Dumas, from Guillumette*

7. *Courtesy of The Most Reverend Richard J. Cushing,*
    Archbishop of Boston

8. *Courtesy of The Most Reverend Richard J. Cushing,*
    Archbishop of Boston

9. *Courtesy of the* Boston Herald

10. *Courtesy of the* Boston Herald

110

E PI